Editor:
HARRY J STEPHAN PhD

Creative Director and Photographer:
KEITH PHILLIPS

Art Director, DTP Design and Layout:
TORGNY JI HYLÉN

Creative Co-ordinator:
JOHN-CLIVE DAWSON-SQUIBB

Proofreader:
TESSA KENNEDY

Illustrator:
LORETTA CHEGWIDDEN

Reproduction by
UNIFOTO INTERNATIONAL (Pty) Ltd
Cape Town

Printing and binding by
TIEN WAH PRESS (PTE) Ltd
Singapore

Vasco da Gama:
The Diary of His Travels through African Waters 1497–1499 © 1998
Stephan Phillips (Pty) Ltd
Graphics © 1998
Stephan Phillips (Pty) Ltd

Reg. No. 96/16989/07

ISBN 0-620-22388-X

Stephan Phillips (Pty) Ltd
PO Box 1230
Somerset West 7129

Vasco da Gama

The Diary of His Travels through African Waters

1497 1499

This book was kindly supported with a grant from the Vasco da Gama Museum at Shelley Point.

Contents

Foreword

We are all acquainted with the names of Portugal's great mariners – Dias, da Gama, Cabral and Magellan – and five hundred years after Vasco da Gama rounded the Cape of Good Hope, his voyage still stands as an epic in the annals of discovery.

Although the diary of Vasco da Gama's journey provides an intimate account of the struggle to find the sea route to India, the circumstances surrounding the journey are still fraught with intrigue. Even today scholarship on the subject remains shrouded in mystery. Eric Axelson has worked on the history of Portuguese maritime discovery since the 1930s, and his remarkable insight and notes go far to remove the veil of secrecy that still dominates the issue.

Why, for example, did da Gama sail south-west away from Africa towards Brazil? Surely the Portuguese were already acquainted with the patterns of the trade winds and westerlies that stream through the southern latitudes? More importantly, could Vasco da Gama sail from Portugal to the Cape without taking on water throughout the entire journey? Why is there no record in the diary for the 65 days when Vasco da Gama passed Brazil, and why did the Martellus map depict the Cape at latitudes over 40 degrees South? Vasco da Gama knew that the Cape could be rounded at 35° S. What prompted the Portuguese to turn down Columbus? Did they already know that the sea route to India lay south and not west?

Finding the sea route to India not only gave Portugal access to immense wealth, but also provided a means of flanking the Arab world that held the overland silk route to the East. Lagos and Lisbon must have been teeming with spies who were anxious to learn the Portuguese maritime secrets of the day. Five hundred years later we are beginning to unravel the mystery.

Harry J Stephan

Acknowledgements

The author expresses his deep indebtedness to the following:

Harry Stephan and Keith Phillips for producing this book.

The Biblioteca Estense Universitaria, Modena, for permitting the printing of the 'Cantino' map in full and in parts.

The Künstistorisches Museum, Vienna, for permission to print the presumed portrait of João II.

Directors of the Imprensa Nacional/Casa da Moeda for permission to use – as far as lies in their power – material published in *Portvgaliae Monvmenta Cartographica*, in 1960 and 1987.

Comandante Joaquim Soeiro de Brito for permission to use illustrations that have appeared in publications of the Comissao Nacional dos Descobrimentos Portugueses.

The Museu Nacional de Arte Antiga, the Arquivo Nacional da Torre do Tombo and the Biblioteca Nacional for permission to publish pictures and documents, and the Arquivo Nacional de Fotografia for actual photographs.

M van Wyk Smith for permitting publication of poetry that appeared in *Shades of Adamastor.*

Prof. Guy Butler for permission to print stanzas from his translation of Camoes' *Lusiados.*

The Campbell Library of the University of Natal for permission to publish poems by Roy Campbell.

And I acknowledge my indebtedness to the masters who wrote on the Portuguese Discoveries, especially Damião Peres, and my friends Armando Cortesão and Avelino Teixeira da Mota.

Eric Axelson

*Vasco da Gama's
probable route in
1497, as visualised by
Gago Coutinho in 1940.
The red line is Vasco da Gama's
outward bound journey. The yellow
portion, off the bulge of Brazil,
indicates Gago Coutinho's later
conviction that Vasco da Gama saw
and probably landed on the Brazilian
coast. The green line is da Gama's
homeward voyage from India.*

Cape Cross padrão, from a cast in the South African Cultural History Museum, Cape Town.

Introduction

Vasco da Gama commanded the first vessels to sail from Europe to India. This voyage revolutionised trade and relations between Europe and the East. Until then valuable products of the East went westwards via land routes to the Black Sea, or up the Persian Gulf or Red Sea, towards the eastern Mediterranean. Venetians were particularly active in distributing these expensive silks and spices through the Strait of Gibraltar to northern Europe. This traffic became safer from attack by Moors in Morocco after the capture of Ceuta by Portugal in 1415.

King João I knighted his three eldest sons, Duarte, Pedro and Henrique, on the Ceuta battlefield. The King named Pedro Duke of Coimbra: he became lord of extensive areas stretching from Coimbra down the Mondego River to its mouth, where he fostered maritime developments.

Pedro travelled extensively in Europe between 1425 and 1429. He visited London and Oxford, Flanders, Central Europe, and the Balkans. He and his accompanying cavaliers fought against invading Turks, and reached the Black Sea. He distinguished himself on the Marches of Treviso, and was warmly welcomed in Italian towns, especially in Venice.

In Venice Pedro met cartographers; he visited shipyards and would have seen caravels being built. And he learnt much about international trade, including that with the East.

Familiar with the classics, he would have discussed with Venetian cartographers Herodotus's description of the circumnavigation of Africa by Phoenicians about 600 BC. This was feasible, taking into account monsoons, trade-winds and harvest times – including a possible harvest on the shore of St Helena Bay.

In Venice Pedro would have heard of the two Vivaldi brothers, merchants of Genoa, who set out in two galleys from Genoa in 1291, in order to reach India by the Ocean Sea, to bring back trade goods. They reached Cape Nun, on the Moroccan coast, but were not heard of again.

Several medieval maps showed Africa as surrounded by water. Pedro brought back with him to Portugal a chart, probably by Andrea Bianco, and a manuscript copy of the book by Marco Polo, the Venetian trader-traveller, who in 1272 reached China, served the Kublai Khan on a number of missions, and returned in 1298 to Venice. It was probably Pedro who translated his book into Portuguese: it deepened his interest in the East.

João I died in 1433. Duarte succeeded; but he died in 1438. The heir, Afonso V, was a child, and in 1439 Pedro became regent. Pedro ruled until 1446 when Afonso V reached his majority (at the age of 14). Pedro's international outlook and his attempts to modernise the government of Portugal, and restrict the treasonable powers of feudal lords, instigated by the house of Bragança, led to his bloody death in 1449. Before his death he ordered a world map from cartographers in Venice. This Fra Mauro map embodied maritime discoveries up to 1448. It reached Portugal only in 1459, after the final payment to craftsmen and artist was made. It was a gigantic circular wallhanging, nearly 2 metres in diameter. It showed a shortened Africa; Ethiopia in great detail; and off the south-eastern coast a channel, with the long island of Diab (Madagascar) beyond. The map in Portugal disappeared in the 18th century but a copy – or the original – survives in Venice.

OGS Crawford in *Ethiopian Itineraries circa 1400–1524* (Hakluyt Society, London, 1958, pp. 16–18) wrote: 'Fra Mauro's map, though not without some Ptolemaic allusions, embodied the best and most up-to-date information about Africa which was available in Venice in the years preceding its completion on 20 August 1460 ... The Ethiopian portion is particularly good; ... and was based upon maps drawn for him by religious persons born in Ethiopia ... That Fra Mauro also used Arab sources is obvious from the places he marks along the east coast of Africa, facing the Indian Ocean ...' including Sofala. 'Fra Mauro shows Africa surrounded on the west, south and east by the ocean. That was what was believed in his time and for at least 170 years before.' 'This world map ... is one of the most beautiful ever drawn.'

It was this Fra Mauro map, Alfredo Pinheiro Marques has forcefully argued, that sparked the Plan of India – for Portugal to explore round the south of Africa and discover the sea route to India. It was Pedro's grandson, King João II, who executed the plan.

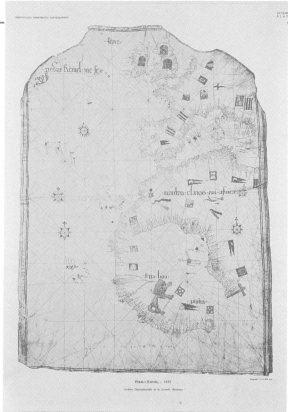

*Map by Pedro Reinel, c. 1495, in Archives
Départementales de la Gironde, Bordeaux.
From Portvgaliae Monvmenta Cartographica,
1960, Plate 521.*

Pedro delegated supervision of exploration down the bulge of Africa to his brother Henrique, but by the time of Henrique's death in 1460 Portuguese vessels had reached only to Serra Leóa. In 1468 Afonso V granted a monopoly of the commerce of Guinea to a Lisbon merchant on condition that he discover 100 leagues of coastline a year. The incentive worked well, and in 1471 caravels reached villages where gold was traded. Exploration reached the equator. Afonso V in 1474 granted control of the Guinea trade to his son João, who came to the throne in 1481. There can be no doubt that the young João II looked far beyond immediate commercial gain. He had from the first firm geopolitical aims to enter into close relations with Prester John, king of Ethiopia, who had sent an embassy to Portugal in 1452. He also wanted to open a Muslim-free route round Africa to India which would produce for Portugal riches of the East to supplement those already being obtained from Guinea. João ordered a fortified trading station to be established on the Gold Coast, and in January 1482 work began on the construction of the fortress of São Jorge de Mina. A brisk trade in gold immediately began; and São Jorge de Mina proved to be a valuable base for further exploration.

In 1482 Diogo Cão reached the mouth of the Congo River, where he raised a padrão – a landmark of Portuguese limestone which consisted of a column surmounted by a cube, above which was a cross. João's coat of arms and an inscription proudly proclaimed Portuguese priority in those waters and Portuguese title. The cross announced the coming of Christianity. On a second expedition in 1486 Cão placed his furthest padrão in latitude 21°47' S on what later came to be Cape Cross, in present-day Namibia. Sight of the North Star had early been lost, but the height of the sun at midday was measured by astrolabes and quadrants, and newly calculated astronomical tables provided latitude.

In 1487 João II ordered Bartolomeu Dias to round Africa. Dias commanded three caravels. At Mina supplies were replenished. The vessel carrying reserve stores was left in a bay on the coast of Angola. No contemporary documents of the voyage survive, but the 16th century chronicler Barros wrote that in January 1488 they came to the 'bay called das Voltas because of the many tacks they made in it, which caused them to give it this name, Bartolomeu Dias being detained there five days by weather which did not allow him to pursue his course, which bay is in south latitude 29°. Having set out from this bay, steering seaward the same weather drove them for 13 days with their sails at half mast, and as the vessels were small and the sea colder and no longer like those of the land of Guinea … they expected these to prove fatal; but the weather which caused this furious sea ceasing, they made for land, steering to the east, thinking the coast still ran from north to south as they had found so far. But after sailing some days without reaching it, they steered to the north and thus reached a bay, which they called dos Vaqueiros, because of the many cows which they saw upon the land guarded by their herds'.

At Alexander Bay, in latitude 28°34' S, percentage frequencies of wind at 08.00, 15.00 and 20.00 hours during January are 20 per cent calm; from the north-east and north, 0 per cent; from the north-west, 1 per cent. Obviously the caravels could not have been driven southwards for 13 days by a northerly gale. Winds blow, however, from the south and south-east for 54 per cent of the time. The velocity at 14.00 hours each day averages 19 knots, and gales occur on eight occasions. Obviously Dias tired of beating against the southerlies, and after five frustrating days he deliberately left the coast and tacked south-west for 13 days to about 39°, in which latitude the explorers would have found favourable – and sometimes

The caravel Bartolomeu Dias, *which in 1988 re-enacted Dias's voyage of 1488. Photograph by Captain Emilio de Sousa.*

over-favourable – west winds. Cold fronts are frequent in those latitudes, and sails would have often been reduced as the caravels sailed to the east. (E Axelson, *The Dias Voyage, 1487–1488: Toponymy and Padrões*; Centro de Estudos de História e Cartografia Antiga 189, Lisbon, 1988, pp. 39–40.) Finding no land Dias turned northwards and made landfall near present-day Mossel Bay.

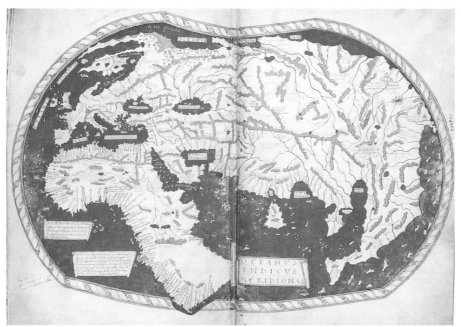

Martellus map (c. 1489). Photograph by the British Museum.

Dias turned at a river he named Rio do Infante, placed a padrão, and discovered and named the Cabo da Boa Esperança, where the pilot, Pero de Alenquer, landed and shot the sun with a terrestrial astrolabe. Approaching Mina, Dias rescued Pacheco Pereira, who had lost his vessel while exploring river mouths flowing into the Bight of Biafra. He reached the Tagus at the end of December 1488.

João II summoned Dias to meet Christopher Columbus's brother, Bartolomeu, a map-maker living in Lisbon. Bartolomeu recorded: 'Note that in this year of 88 there arrived in Lisbon Bartolomeu Dias … and he reported to the same Most Serene King how he had navigated 600 leagues beyond where it was already navigated … to a promontory to which he gave the name of Cabo da Boa Esperança, which we judge to be in Abyssinia, which place he found by astrolable to be at a distance of 45° below the equatorial line, and this place is distant from Lisbon 3,100 leagues. This voyage he painted and described league by league on a navigation map for the Most Serene King to see with his own eyes; in all of which I took part.' (A Fontoura da Costa, *Às portas da India em 1484*, Lisbon, 1936, p. 52. Fontoura da Costa added that the 'interfui' in the original Latin and 'tomei parte' in the translation simply meant that Bartolomeu was present at the interview.)

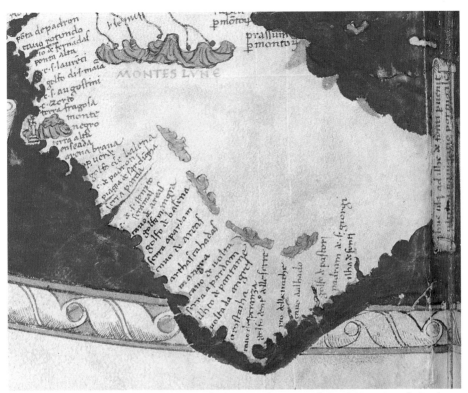

A portion of the Martellus map (c. 1489) showing the Cape of Good Hope in a latitude over 40° S to deter any possible Spanish competition. Dias knew that the Cape of Good Hope was in latitude 35° S [actually 34°51' S]. Photograph by the British Museum.

João II would already have seen Dias's chart, and have known that the Cape of Good Hope was in latitude 35° S. João without doubt ordered Dias to say that it was in 45° to deter any possible Spanish competition.
It was probably Columbus, however, who persuaded Martellus to lengthen Africa in his map from 35° to 45°. In that, João and Columbus were at one. And he encouraged Columbus in his scheme to sail westward to the East. Dias's nautical advisers knew that Columbus was vastly underestimating the size of the globe.

Dias had rounded Africa. He had sailed to where the coast was trending to the north-east, and to where there was a strong warm current flowing from the north-east. He had definitely reached the Indian Ocean.

It would have been natural for João to plan further maritime exploration immediately on Dias's return, but he was awaiting the arrival of reports from two agents despatched, also in 1487, to travel to the Middle East by way of the Mediterranean. Pero da Covilhã had served Afonso V and then João II as espionage agent and squire of war. He had spent most of three years on commercial and diplomatic missions to Morocco where he acquired knowledge of Arabic language and customs. He was to visit India and learn all he could about the spice trade, which was known to be largely in the hands of Muslim traders who would naturally resent the intrusion of Christian competitors. João accordingly sent as Covilhã's companion another squire, Afonso de Paiva, who was also a master of Arabic, to carry a letter to Prester John – considered to be a potential ally – to enquire whether his empire extended to the east African shore. Covilhã was also to enquire about maritime conditions on the east African coast.

In Cairo the two agents had the good fortune to meet some Arabs from Morocco, and in their company sailed to Aden. There they parted company, Paiva making for Abyssinia, Covilhã for India. Covilhã correctly assessed the importance of Calicut, in the Malabar Coast, as the pivotal centre of the spice trade. He sailed to Hormuz, at the entrance to the Persian Gulf, and from there boarded a vessel sailing down the east African coast. He visited Kilwa, Malindi, Mombasa and Moçambique, and reached Sofala, from where gold from inland Monomotapa was exported. He visited Mecca, and returned to Cairo at the end of 1490 or the beginning of 1491. There he and Paiva were due to meet, and return together to Portugal. He learnt to his distress that Paiva had died without reaching Ethiopia. Two emissaries from João II passed on instructions that the two agents were not to return until they had completed their missions. It was particularly important to open communication with Prester John. Covilhã wrote a lengthy report detailing his journeys, and included a map of their situation. He then dutifully made his way to the main port of entry to Abyssinia. At the court of the Negus he was very well received. He was given a wife and other possessions – and refused permission to depart. He was able to give encyclopaedic information about Ethiopia to a Portuguese diplomatic mission when it arrived in 1520.

Covilhã's report could have reached João at the end of 1491 or the beginning of 1492. Still unexplored was the comparatively short stretch of African coastline from the Rio do Infante to Sofala. João would have stepped up exploration of the western Atlantic to ensure fair winds for a different class of vessel called *naus*, which were square-rigged ships that required following winds for successful sailing. However, a distraction from his plan soon arose.

Portugal and Castile had warred over possession of the Canary Islands and adjacent mainland in 1478. At the end of the war, in the treaty of Alcáçovas, Portugal surrendered her claims and obtained a line of latitude through the southernmost extremity of the Canaries – here, on 27°30' N – as the boundary between their activities. About the same time Cristóbal Colon, as Columbus preferred to be called, landed on the Portuguese shore. In the period between 1480 and 1485 'Christopher Columbus marries a daughter of the late Bartolomeu Perestrelo, donatory of the small island of Porto Santo. He spends some years there and in Madeira. His mother-in-law gives him her late husband's maps and documents. He travels the Portuguese routes to Guinea and the Western Atlantic, gathering information about the Portuguese discoveries and acquiring the knowledge of seafaring which was to help him bring his plan to sail to the West to maturity.' (Pinheiro Marques, *Portugal and the Discovery of the Atlantic*, Lisbon, 1990, p. 99.)

Armando Cortesão commented: 'When he had been informed of what Columbus really was doing, D. João II encouraged him in his project of reaching the Orient by sailing westwards, where he knew that some lands would be found. He did so because he rightly expected to divert the attention of the Spaniards from his well advanced plan of reaching India by sailing round the African continent. Columbus was cleverly used by the shrewd Portuguese King as a tool to help him in the execution of his vast plan of discoveries ... Columbus was to some extent, either consciously or unconsciously, a sophisticated tool in the plan of discoveries.' (*The Mystery of Vasco da Gama*, Coimbra, 1973, pp. 83, 88.)

João II naturally refused to support Columbus, and the Spanish monarchs considered his demands for rewards if successful to be preposterous. Eventually, in 1492, he sailed from Palos, and found beautiful islands in the Bahamas, and the coast of a large island which, he declared, was Cipango (Japan): it was Cuba. On his return it is significant, perhaps, that he took his wind-battered *Niña* not directly to Palos but first to the Tagus. He was hospitably received, and had two interviews with João at Val-do-Paraíso. The *Niña* was supplied with everything she needed, and after a week's stay she sailed on 13 March 1493 for Palos.

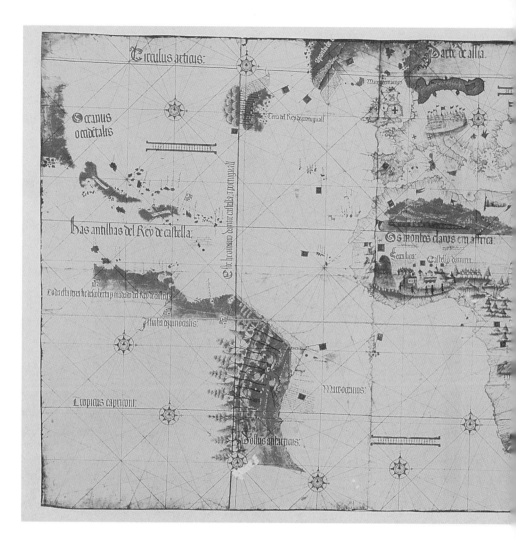

João II promptly protested to the Spanish monarchs that the lands found by Columbus were in the Portuguese zone, as defined in the treaty of Alcáçovas, and let it be known that he was organising a squadron to take possession of these lands.

Certainly the Portuguese had for many years explored the western Atlantic. Madeira, rediscovered in 1420, had provided an admirable base for exploration southwards, but there was difficulty in returning against

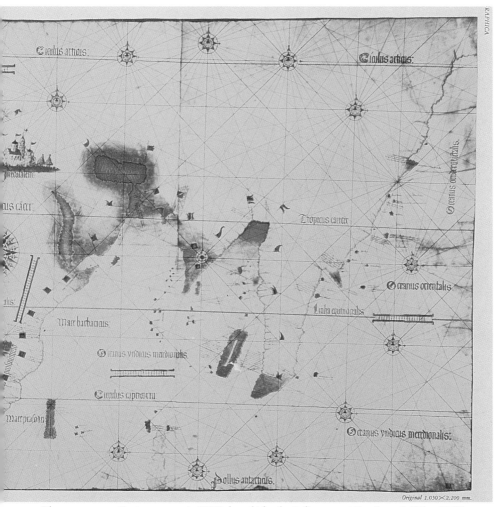

The anonymous Portuguese map, 1502, bought by the Italian agent Cantino. 1 051 x 2 200 mm. In Biblioteca Estense Universitaria, Modena.

prevailing north and north-west winds. Pizzigano's map of the Atlantic of 1424 had marked the Açores, and returning vessels were now able to strike towards those islands when they found favourable winds from the south and south-west, especially in the winter. The map marked two large islands to the west of the Açores, one of which was called Antilia. According to Portuguese tradition Christian refugees had fled from the Iberian peninsula when it was over-run by Moors in the 8th century to Antilia.

A chart of 1435 marked a 'mar de baga' – the Sargasso sea: 'The Portuguese must have already reached these distant longitudes (the Central Atlantic) during the course of the detours they took on their return from the African coast to avoid the north-easterlies and to catch the favourable westerly winds which prevail in the latitudes of the Açores.' (Pinheiro Marques, *Portvgaliae Monvmenta Cartographica, Vol. VI, Adenda,* Lisbon, 1987, p. 50.)

Later maps of the 15th century showed an Island of Seven Cities west of the Açores. Teles de Meneses tried during 1474 and 1475 to find the island. In 1486 João II authorised an Açorean, Dulmo, and a Madeiran, do Estreito, to make voyages of exploration in the western Atlantic, and Dulmo was granted concession of all inhabited islands and mainlands he found.

João II was right in his claim that the newly found islands were in his zone. The northernmost point Columbus reached was at about 24° N and the Portuguese zone extended to 27°30' N.

The Catholic sovereigns requested the Pope to issue a Bull declaring that the lands found by Columbus were their property. Alexander VI was, according to EG Ravenstein (quoted in Armando Cortesão, *Mystery*, p. 151), 'the most memorable of the corrupt and secular popes of the Renaissance ... the pope himself shamelessly cast aside all decorum, living a purely secular and immoral life ... ever intriguing, ready to ally himself with whichever power promised at the moment most advantageous terms'. The third Bull issued accepted a proposal by Columbus that there be a new line of division of spheres, a line of longitude, running 100 leagues west of the Açores or Cape Verde islands. João II refused to accept this line. In 1492 Spanish forces had occupied Granada, the last stronghold of Moors – and Ferdinand and Isabella had married. Exiled members of the house of Bragança in Castile urged the monarchs to invade and conquer Portugal, but good sense prevailed, and negotiations began between the two countries. Pacheco Pereira was particularly active in securing in the Treaty of Tordesilhas, 1494, a line of longitude 370 leagues west of the Cape Verde islands as the delimitation between the spheres of activity.

The 370 line west of the Cape Verde islands descended to meet the equator at right angles, and then extended northwards and southwards. Avelino Teixeira da Mota showed that much depended on the projection used: in one the line passed through the bulge of Brazil from about 1° S, and to

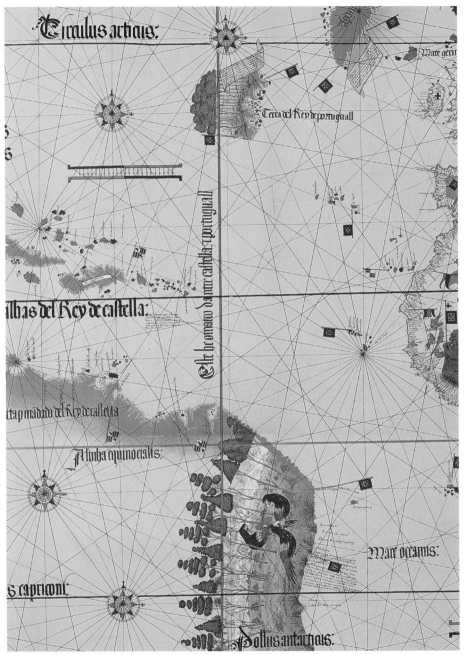

A section of the 'Cantino' map showing the bulge of Brazil and the Tordesilhas Line.

Greenland. In another the line passed further down Brazil to about 33° S, and included Tierra del Fuego and Labrador. The line was to cause much controversy in the 16th century, but did guarantee Portugal's command of the vital western South Atlantic.

Armando Cortesão pointed out that the treaty line gave another great advantage to Portugal: João's nautical advisers informed him that the 370 league line, extended by 180°, would place Malacca, strategic port midway between the East and the Far East, and the spice-rich Moluccas in the Portuguese sphere.

Gago Coutinho, an experienced sailor and navigator, showed on a map drawn in 1940, Vasco da Gama's 1497 route as depicted by Kopke and Ravenstein. Coutinho also considered this route to be the most probable between Serra Leóa and St Helena Bay. He showed Vasco da Gama passing about 50 miles from Pernambuco (in 8°04' S). In the *Diário da Viagem de Vasco da Gama* (Vol. II, 1945, pp. 103–104), he declared firmly that the practicality of finding a route across the Atlantic would not have been found at the first attempt by chance: it must have been the result of reconnaissances between 1487 and 1497. In *A Náutica dos Descobrimentos: Os Descobrimentos Marítimos vistos por um navegador, Colectânea* (Vol. II, p. 94), he insisted that by the signing of the Tordesilhas treaty there must have been Portuguese knowledge not only of the western South Atlantic but also of the flanking land in Brazil, from Cape São Roque to Cape Santo Agostinho. There must too have been exploratory voyages at various times in the year because Vasco da Gama's voyage and Cabral's official discovery in 1500 were at different seasons of the year.

Little is known about the planning of the Vasco da Gama expedition because of the disappearance of Chancery documents from 1492 to 1495 (and of 1485). It has been assumed that they were destroyed by henchmen of King Manuel (who came to the throne in 1495), who was bitterly jealous of João's achievements. Sad too was the destruction in Lisbon's 1755 earthquake and fire of the Guinea and Mina records. Among the documents in the National Archives that survived are some containing details of the issue of ship's biscuits to certain vessels of the later 15th century. Most of these papers supply the names of the master or pilot, the number of crew, and the weight of the biscuit supplied, which was approximately 1 kg per man per day.

One day in August 1489 enough biscuit was loaded aboard an unidentified vessel, 'to be delivered to whom our lord the King will say', to feed the crew of two caravels, each with 40 men aboard, for two years and one month. The destination was not given. This, and several similar supplies, were doubtless for exploration westwards in the South Atlantic – and perhaps an attempt to close the gap between Rio do Infante and Sofala.

On 22 April 1500 Cabral's fleet came within sight of land, and on 25 April the vessels anchored in Porto Seguro. There is some documentary evidence of a pre-Cabral discovery of Brazil. King Manuel's physician/surgeon/ astronomer Mestre João wrote to the king from this newly discovered land of Vera Cruz, which he placed in latitude 17° S, telling him that if he wished to know the situation of this land the King should ask to have brought to him the world-map which Pero Vaz Bisagudo (captain of an expedition sent to Senegal) received: but this did not note whether the land was inhabited or not – it was a 'mapa antiga', an old map. (A Fontoura da Costa, *O Descobrimento do Brasil*, Lisbon, 1961, off-print, no pagination.)

Manuel, in a letter to the monarchs of Spain written on 28 August 1501, referred to the land 'novamente' discovered by Cabral (*História da Colonização Portuguesa do Brasil*, Vol. II, Porto, 1923, p. 165). Michaelis translates 'novamente' as 'again, once more, newly, afresh, over, over and over again'.

The publication of TA Chumovsky's *Três Roteiros Desconhecidos de Ahmad ibn-Madjid O Piloto Árabe de Vasco da Gama* in 1957 caused excitement, reporting as it did an unknown Portuguese expedition to Sofala in about AD 1494, and naming the pilot who took Vasco da Gama's squadron so accurately from Malindi to Calicut. Ibrahim Khoury, however, made a deep study in verse of those rutters, of Sofala. In *As-Sufaliyya "The poem of Sofala" by Ahmad ibn Magid* (Centro de Estudos de Cartografia Antiga, CXLVIII, Coimbra, 1983), he found that of the 807 verses, 106 had been posthumously and falsely inserted, including those which referred to the Franks (the Portuguese), and Madjid being Gama's pilot.

There is, however, further evidence of a possible Portuguese expedition to east Africa before 1498: the so-called Cantino map, bought by the Italian agent in Lisbon at the end of October 1502. Armando Cortesão established that none of the three fleets arriving in Lisbon before 1503 stayed long enough in African waters to make such a detailed hydrographical survey of east Africa as was shown on the map. 'How then to explain the near perfection of the representation of Africa in that planisphere, which implies a careful survey. The only explanation is that it cannot be but the result of unknown earlier voyages, therefore prior to Vasco da Gama's expedition of 1497.' (*Mystery*, pp. 111–112, followed by 20 pages of maps and lists of place names.)

Pacheco Pereira, in a work written between 1505 and 1508, a time when one was compelled to laud King Manuel, was obviously referring to João II when he recorded that 'our lord the King ordered the construction of four ships, the largest not to exceed a hundred tons, for the land being utterly unknown it was unnecessary that they should be larger. The reason was that they might be able to enter and leave any place on the coast easily, which they could not do if they were larger. They were built by excellent masters and workmen, with strong nails and wood; each ship had three sets of sails and anchors and three or four times as much other tackle and rigging as was usual. The cooperage of the casks, pipes and barrels for wine, water, vinegar and oil was strengthened with many hoops of iron. The provisions of bread, wine, flour, meat, vegetables, medicines, and likewise of arms and ammunition, were also in excess of what was needed for such a voyage. The best and most skilful pilots and mariners in Portugal were sent on this voyage.' (G Kimble, trans. and ed., *Esmeraldo de Situ Orbis*, Hakluyt Society, 1937, p. 166.)

João II chose Vasco da Gama to lead the expedition. Castanheda, the most trustworthy of the 16th-century chroniclers, declared that João had selected him because he was 'experienced in nautical matters and had done the King João II good service at sea'. AC Teixeira wrote a comprehensive book on the life of *Vasco da Gama e a Vidigueira* (Lisbon, 1898) but found Gama's only known contact with the sea before 1497 was in 1492, seizing some French vessels in the Portuguese port of Setubal. It is significant that João II, shortly before his death, ordered that Vasco da Gama be awarded two commanderies 'considering the many services that Vasco da Gama, a fidalgo of the household of the King ... has rendered to him ... and in the hope that he will render in the future'. He had obviously headed expeditions before 1497, possibly to Sofala or to the western South Atlantic.

Vasco da Gama sailed from the Tagus in 1497 as 'captão-mor' of four vessels. There were beautiful paintings of three of these in *Livro de Lisuarte de Abreu* (Lisbon, 1992), but the order to make pictorial records of all armadas that went to India was given only in 1536. There is an equally attractive picture of four vessels in 'Livro das Armadas' in the Academia das Ciências de Lisboa, but this was painted c. 1568. No contemporary picture of the vessels is in existence.

Jaime Martins Barata researched the probable features of Gama's flagship and other contemporary naus (*O Navio "São Gabriel" e as Naus Manuelinas*, Agrupamento de Estudos de Cartografia Antiga (AECA), Vol. XXXIX, Coimbra, 1970). He studied, in the absence of contemporary pictures, the earliest known printed pictures of late 15th- and 16th-century naus. In 1496 'Valentin of Moravia' printed *História do Imperador Vespasiono* with a woodblock of a ship with a large square sail on the mainmast, which was surmounted by a top, a small lateen sail on a foremast in the prow, and two lateen sails on two short masts on the poop (*História da Colonização Portuguesa do Brasil*, Vol. I, 1921, p. 20.) The same block was used by Valentim Fernandes on the title-page of his *Marco Polo, Lisbon, 1502.* (Armando Cortesão, *History of Portuguese Cartography*, I, Coimbra, 1969, p. 287.)

Barata, after studying early Portuguese books, charts and nautical guides, produced a drawing of a possible 22 m long ship, with a great square mainsail on the mainmast, a small square sail on a short mast in the prow, and a small lateen sail on a mizzen rising from the poop. One sheet of the Abreu collection is particularly interesting. This purports to show the armadas of 1502. Manuel sent Vasco da Gama in overall command of the three armadas. One of his orders was to wage war on Calicut. But the Abreu artist showed Vasco da Gama's nau not as the largest and most heavily gunned vessel but with a single mainmast carrying one large mainsail. The artist might perhaps have been given a confused recollection of the rigging of Gama's vessel on his first voyage.

Chroniclers of the 18th century exaggerated the tonnage of these four vessels. Preferable are the statements of two contemporary observers. According to Pacheco Pereira not one of the ships exceeded 100 tons. Girolamo Sernigi, a Florentine merchant, was in Lisbon when the two surviving vessels of the expedition returned to the Tagus. He recorded that the two naus had been of 90 tons, the provision ship of 110 tons, and the caravel of 50 tons. There are differences of opinion as to how the Portuguese ton of the time compares with the metric ton of today. According to Humberto Leitão and Vicente Lopes (*Dicionário da Linguagem de Marinha Antiga e Actual*, Lisbon, 1974), it was equivalent to 793 kg.

Vasco da Gama's flagship was the nau *São Gabriel*; his elder brother, Paulo, commanded the nau *São Rafael*; Nicolau Coelho commanded the caravel *Berrio*; and Gonçalo Nunes the storeship (a nau). The chief pilot was Pero de Alenquer.

The so-called 'Diário' that follows is the only contemporary record of Vasco da Gama's historic voyage. It is, unfortunately, not a true diary, 'a daily record of events'. Days, and even weeks, intervene between some entries. It is unfortunate too that the 'diary' is not the original document made by the diarist, but by a copyist in the 16th century. This copy came to light in the convent of Santa Cruz in Coimbra. It entered the Biblioteca Publica of Porto. It was first edited by Diogo Kopke, professor of mathematics, and António da Costa Paiva, professor of botany and agriculture, at the Academia Polytechnica of Porto, and published in 1838, thanks to contributions made by 274 subscribers whose names appear in the book.

The editors named the book *Roteiro da Viagem que em Descobrimento da India Pelo Cabo da Boa Esperança fez Dom Vasco da Gama em 1497*. It was not a 'roteiro', a rutter, because it did not detail routes. Vasco da Gama reached India not in 1497 but in 1498. And he was not Dom until 1499.

The anonymous diarist mentioned that he was present when Vasco da Gama disembarked at Calicut to meet the Samorim. Castanheda, who had read the 'diary', gave the names of 12 Portuguese who accompanied Vasco da Gama. Kopke (pp. xv–xvi) eliminated 11 of these as possible authors, which left Álvaro Velho as the most likely.

Valentim Fernandes was asked by a group of merchants in Germany to send them information about the Guinea coast. This he did, in documents mainly of 1506 and 1507 and some of 1508. One of those of 1508 declared that idol-worshipping (i.e. non-Muslim) inhabitants were found south of Serra

Leóa and trustworthy information about them and their environment had been contributed by Álvaro Velho, who had been in that area for eight years. Álvaro Velho was from Barreira. Barreira was across the Tagus from Lisbon. He would certainly have known Alcochete, 10 miles up the Tagus. And the diarist had a happy reference to Alcochete.

This possible identification was made by Franz Hümmerich (*Vasco da Gama und die Entdeckung des Seewegs nach Ostindien*, München, 1898), who added a possible explanation for the abrupt termination of the diary on the shoals off Rio Grande: that Álvaro Velho was a 'degredado', a man banished for a crime, who, in the absence of a royal pardon, preferred to live in Guinea.

Luís de Albuquerque (*Relação da Viagem de Vasco da Gama Álvaro Velho*, Lisbon, 1989, pp. 5, 6) accepted that this identification was 'strongly probable', and the degredado suggestion though purely 'conjectural' was 'very probable'.

The diary was translated into elegant English and edited by EG Ravenstein: *Vasco da Gama's First Voyage*, Hakluyt Society, London, 1898. CD Ley reproduced the 'Route to India' in *Portuguese Voyages 1498–1663*, London, 1947, pp. 1–38. The section of the diary covering from Mossel Bay to Moçambique appeared in Portuguese, and in English translated by Freire de Andrade, in *Documentos sobre os Portugueses em Moçambique e na Africa Central* ... I, Lisbon, 1962, pp. 3–27.

The editor for *South African Explorers*, Oxford, 1954, translated the diary as far as Moçambique somewhat more literally in places than Ravenstein. He used the excellent *Diário da Viagem de Vasco da Gama*, Porto, 1945, which contained a facsimile of the manuscript, plus a transcription into modern form. Volume I was introduced by Damião Peres. Volume II contained valuable notes, especially by Gago Coutinho. This translation has been revised in places and extended to cover the crossing to India, and the return voyage. Very helpful has been Leitão & Lopes, *Dicionário*. In the present translation paragraphing has been modified in the interests of readability, and many 'Items' and 'ands' have been omitted. King Manoel's name has been modernised to Manuel.

Reputed portrait of King João II, in the Künsthistorisches Museum, Vienna.

The illustration is from Alfredo Pinheiro Marques's Vida e Obra do 'Principe Perfeito' Dom João II, *Figueira da Foz, 1997.*

The lettering in the background is [JOH]ANNES QVARTUS R[EY] [POR]TVGLIA R, i.e. John the 4th of Portugal.

Asked to explain the apparent discrepancy in the numbers, Alfredo Marques replied that 'King João II had close family relations with Emperor Maximilian, and certainly when the portrait was made the Austrians didn't know very much about Portuguese history and the erroneous lettering was included because they thought that João II was the fourth Portuguese King (instead of no. 13). The probable reason for that was the fact that he was the FOURTH King of the Dinastia de Avis, the Portuguese Dynasty most well known in Europe.'

The Diary

In the name of God, Amen.

In the year 1497 King Dom Manuel, the first of this name in Portugal, ordered four vessels to go and discover, in search of spices. Vasco da Gama went as Commander-in-Chief of these vessels. Paulo da Gama, his brother, captained one, and Nicolau Coelho another.

We left from Restelo[1] one Saturday, the 8th day of July of the said year, 1497, on our journey. May God our Lord allow us to complete it in His service, Amen.

Firstly, we arrived the following Saturday within sight of the Canaries,[2] and that night we passed to leeward of Lançarote. In the following night, at break of day, we found ourselves off the Terra Alta where we fished for about two hours and this night, as soon as it grew dusk, we were off the Rio do Ouro.

During the night the fog was so dense that Paulo da Gama lost all the fleet by going one way and the Commander-in-Chief another. After it grew light we had sight of neither him nor the other vessels; and we set course for the islands of Cape Verde, as we had been ordered that any who lost company should follow this route.

On Sunday following, as it grew light, we had sight of the island of Sal, and just an hour later we had sight of three vessels. We stood over to them, and found the supply-ship, and Nicolau Coelho, and Bartolomeu Dias who was going in our company to Mina; they too had lost the Commander-in-Chief. After joining together we followed our route; and the wind died on us, and we were becalmed until Wednesday morning. At ten o'clock of that day we had sight of the Commander-in-Chief about five leagues[3] ahead of us and by the close of afternoon we came, with much happiness, to have speech with him; and we fired many bombards[4] and played on trumpets from our great pleasure that we had found him.

On the next day, which was Thursday, we reached the island of Santiago, where with much pleasure and rejoicing we anchored off the beach of Santa Maria. There we took in meats and water and wood, and did needed repairs to yards of our vessels.

One Thursday, which was the 3rd day of August, we left, sailing eastwards[5] and going one day, the 18th day of August, southwards, about 200 leagues from the island of Santiago, the Commander-in-Chief's [main] yard broke; and we lay to under the foresail and lower mainsail[6] for two days and a night.

On the 22nd of the said month, going on a tack out to sea to the south by west,[7] we found many birds resembling herons, and when night came they took off to the south-south-east very strongly like birds going to land. On this same day we saw a whale, and this a good 800 leagues out to sea.[8]

Diário, 1497, p. 3, recording arrival in St Helena Bay.

On the 27th day of the month of October, the eve of St Simon and Judas, which was Friday, we observed many whales and sea-wolves, and what are called quoquas.[9]

One Wednesday, the 1st day of the month of November, which was the day of All Saints, we found many signs of land, which were some 'golfãos' which grow along the coast.[10]

On the 4th day of the month, Saturday, two hours before dawn, we found depth of 110 fathoms[11] at most, and at 9 o'clock of the day we had sight of land. We then all joined together and saluted the Commander-in-Chief with many flags and standards and bombard shots, and all donned festival clothes. This same day when close to land, we tacked out to sea, for we had no recognition of the land.

On Tuesday we came to tack towards the land, and had sight of low land, which had a great bay. The Commander-in-Chief sent Pero de Alenquer in a boat to sound and see if good anchorage could be found. He found it to be very good, with a clean bottom, and sheltered form all winds except the north-west; it lies east and west. To the bay they gave the name Santa Helena.[12]

On Wednesday we cast anchor in the said bay; and here we were for eight days, careening the vessels, repairing the sails and taking in fire-wood.

Four leagues in this bay to the south-east lies a river. It comes from the interior and at its mouth it is a stone's throw across, and two or three fathoms deep at any state of the tide. It is called the Santiago.[13]

In this land the men are swarthy.[14] They eat only sea-wolves and whales and the flesh of gazelles and the roots of plants. They go about covered in skins, and they wear some sheaths on their genitals. Their arms are staffs of wild olive trees tipped with fire-treated horns. They have many dogs like those of Portugal and they bark the same as they do. The birds of this land are also the same as those of Portugal: cormorants, gulls, turtle-doves, larks, and many other birds. The land is very healthy and temperate, and with good herbage.

On the next day after we had anchored, which was Thursday, we went ashore with the Commander-in-Chief and took one of those men. He was small of body and looked like Sancho Mexia. He was going about gathering honey in the heath, for the bees of that land place it at the foot of the scrub. We took him to the Commander-in-Chief's ship, who placed him at his table, and he ate of everything that we ate. The next day the Commander-in-Chief clothed him very well and ordered him to be put ashore. On the following day 14 or 15 of them came to where we had the vessels. The Commander-in-Chief went ashore and showed them many trade-goods to learn if there were such goods in that land; and the goods were cinnamon and cloves, seed-pearls and gold, and other things as well. They did not know those trade-goods at all; it seemed they had never seen them. The Commander-in-Chief gave them little bells and rings of tin.

Vasco da Gama

The Diary of His Travels through African Waters 1497–1499

This was on Friday, and the same on the following Saturday. On Saturday there came about 40 or 50 of them, and we, after dining, went ashore. With ceitis[15] that we carried with us we traded for shells which they wore in their ears, which looked as they had been silvered over, and fox-tails they carry fastened to sticks with which they fan the face. Here I traded a sheath, which one of them wore on his genitals for a ceitil. From this it seemed to us that they prize copper; and they even wore some small beads of it in their ears.

This same day one Fernão Veloso, who went with the Commander-in-Chief, much desired to go

Astrolabe, 1555; silver miniature by Leitão & Leitão, Lisbon.

with them to their houses to learn in what manner they live and what they eat and what their life was like. He begged the Commander-in-Chief as a favour to give him permission to go with them to their houses. The Commander-in-Chief, seeing that he would not stop importuning him until he gave his permission, let him go with them. We returned to the Commander-in-Chief's vessel to sup; and he went with the said negroes.

Soon after they left us they took a sea-wolf, and went to the foot of a hill, a barren place, and roasted the sea-wolf and gave of it to Fernão Veloso who went with them, and roots of plants which they eat. When eating was finished, they told him he should return to the vessels and they did not wish him to go with them. The said Fernão Veloso, as soon as he came opposite the vessels, began to shout, and the men remained concealed in the bush. We were still at supper. As soon as we heard him the captains at once left off eating, and we with them, and threw ourselves into a sailboat. The negroes began to run along the beach and they came as close to the said Fernão Veloso as we were. As we were trying to pick him up they began to attack us with some assagais they carried with them, wounding the Commander-in-Chief and three or four men. This was because we trusted them, they appearing to be of so little courage who would not dare to attack us in the way they did, for which reason we had gone ashore scorning arms. We then took ourselves back to the vessels.

Use of an astrolabe, Duarte Leite, História dos Descobrimentos, *1958, p. 410.*

As soon as we had set our vessels in order and careened them,[16] and taken in firewood we departed from this land, one Thursday, the 16th day of November, in the morning. We did not know how far we were from the Cape of Good Hope, except that Pero de Alenquer said that the most we could be would be 30 leagues short of the Cape.[17] Why he could not be certain was because he had left from the Cape one morning and had passed there at night with the wind astern, and on the outward voyage they had passed by out at sea, and for these reasons he was not able to recognize where we were.

We accordingly tacked out to sea, to the south-south-east,[18] and on Saturday, in the afternoon, we had sight of the said Cape of Good Hope. This same day we stood out on a tack to sea and that night we turned on a landward tack. On Sunday, the 19th day of November, in the morning, we were once again level with the Cape, but we were not able to round it, because the wind was south-south-east, and the said Cape lies north-east and south-west.[19] The same day we turned and tacked out to sea; and on Monday night we returned on a landward tack. That Wednesday at midday we passed the said Cape and sailed along the coast with the wind astern.

Alongside this Cape of Good Hope, to the south, lies a very large bay which enters a good six leagues into the land, its mouth another good six leagues in width.[20]

On the 25th day of the said month November, one Saturday, the day of St Catherine, in the afternoon, we entered the bay of São Bras[21] where we were for 13 days, for there we dismantled the ship that was carrying provisions after transferring them to the other vessels.

On the following Friday, while we were still in the said bay of São Bras, there came about 90 men, swarthy like those of St Helena Bay; and some of them moved about on the beach and others of them remained on the hills. At this time we were all, or the greater part of us, in the Commander-in-Chief's ship. When we saw them we went ashore in the boats, which we armed very well. When we were close to land the Commander-in-Chief threw little bells on to the beach for them, and they took not only those that were thrown to them, but they approached to take them from the hand of the Commander-in-Chief, at which we marvelled greatly, for when Bartolomeu Dias was here they fled from him and would not take anything

Wood-block by Hans Burgkmair, published in 1509, based on description by Balthasar Springer at present-day Plettenberg Bay, in Andrew Smith and WE Pasche, 'Balthasar Springer at the Cape (1506)', Quarterly Bulletin of the South African Library, *March 1997, p. 94.*

from him that he offered them, but rather, one day, as they were taking in water at a very good watering place that is here at the edge of the sea, they defended the watering place with stones thrown from the top of a hill which is above this watering place, and Bartolomeu Dias shot a cross-bow at them and killed one of them. We supposed that they did not flee from us because, it seemed to us, they had news from St Helena Bay (where we first had been), the districts being separated by 60 leagues by sea,[22] that we were men who did not do evil, but even gave things of ours away.

The Commander-in-Chief did not wish to go ashore here because where the negroes were was extensive bush; he changed his position and we went and stopped at another, open, place. Then he landed; and we made signs to the negroes to go to where we were going, and they went. The Commander-in-Chief went ashore, accompanied by men bearing arms, some of them with crossbows. The Commander-in-Chief then ordered them, by signs, to draw away, and that only one or two of them should approach; and to those that came the captain gave little bells and red caps.

They gave us ivory bracelets, which they were wearing on their arms, from which it appears to us that there are many elephants in this land; and we have seen elephant droppings near the watering place where they come to drink.

On Saturday about 200 negroes, large and small, arrived, and brought about 12 head of cattle, oxen and cows, and four or five sheep. When we saw them we went ashore at once. They at once began to play on four or five flutes, and some of them played high and others played low, harmonizing very well for negroes in whom music is not to be expected; and they danced like negroes. The Commander-in-Chief ordered trumpets to be played and we in the boat danced, and so too did the Commander-in-Chief when he rejoined us. When this festa was finished we went ashore where we had been before, and there we traded a black ox for three bracelets. We dined off this on Sunday, and it was very fat; and the flesh of it was as savoury as meat of Portugal.

On Sunday as many men as before arrived, and they brought with them women and youths; the women remained on top of a hillock close to the sea. They brought many oxen and cows; and they put themselves in two places alongside the sea and played and danced as on Saturday. It is the custom of these men for youths to remain in the bush with their arms. The men came to talk with us, carrying some short sticks in their hands and some foxtails fastened to sticks with which they fanned their faces; and while we were talking with them by signs, we saw the youths moving about in the bush, crouching down, and carrying arms in their hands. The Commander-in-Chief ordered a man called Martim Afonso, who had previously travelled in Manicongo,[23] to go forward, and he gave him bracelets to trade for an ox. After they had taken the bracelets they took him by the hand and went to point to the watering place; they asked him why we took their water; and they started to drive the oxen towards the bush. The Commander-in-Chief, when he saw this, ordered us to collect together, and the said Martim Afonso to take shelter, for it seemed to him that they were organising some treachery. Then, when we had collected together, we went to where we had been at first, and they followed us.

The Captain ordered us to go ashore with lances and assagais and crossbows wound, and wearing our breastplates. This was more to show that we were powerful than to do them harm, for this we did not wish to do.

They, when they saw this, started to collect together and run some to the others. The Captain, so that no occasion might be given for killing some of them, ordered us all to regain the boats. After we were all collected together, to give them to understand that we could do them hurt, though we did not wish to do this, he ordered two bombards that were in the stern of the boat to be fired. They were now all seated on the beach adjacent to the bush, but when they heard the discharge of the bombards, they started to flee so briskly to the bush that they dropped the skins with which they were covered, and their arms. After they reached the bush two men returned for these; and they started to join together and to flee to the top of a ridge, driving the cattle before them.

The oxen of this land are very large, like those of Alentejo, and very marvellously fat, and very tame; they are castrated, and some of them do not have horns. The negroes fit the fattest of them with pack-saddles made of boards, like those of Castile, and on top of the pack-saddles some sticks to serve as litters, and they ride on top of them. They thrust a cistus stick through the nostrils of those cattle they wish to barter, and lead them by that.

There is an islet in this bay, three crossbow shots in the sea; and on this islet are many sea-wolves. Some of these are as large as very large bears; they are very frightful, and have very great tusks, and they charge men; and no lance, thrown with whatever force, can wound them.[24] Others are smaller and others very, very small. The big ones roar like lions, and the small ones bleat like kids. We went here one day for diversion, and we saw about 3,000, large and small; and we shot at them from the sea with bombards. There are some birds on this islet, as large as ducks, which do not fly, because they do not have feathers on their wings; they are called fotilicaios, and we killed as many of them as we desired; they bray like asses.[25]

While we were in this bay of São Bras taking in water one Wednesday we placed a cross and a padrão at the said bay of São Bras. We made the cross out of a mizzen-mast, and it was very tall. The following Thursday, as we were about to leave the said bay, before we departed, we saw about 10 or 12 negroes overthrow both the cross and the padrão.[26] After taking in everything that was necessary, we departed from here. This same day we had to anchor again after only two leagues from our place of departure because the wind was light. On Friday, day of our Lady of the Conception, in the morning, we spread our sails and followed on our way. On the Tuesday following, the eve of Santa Lucia, we had a violent storm, and we ran with the wind astern and a greatly lowered foresail. On this route we lost Nicolau Coelho, in the morning. When it came to sunset they saw him from the main-yard, astern from us four or five leagues. It seemed to us that he had seen us. We showed signal lights, and lay to. At the end of the first watch he came up with us, not because he had seen us during the day, but because we were sailing close to the wind and there was nothing he could do but follow in our wake.

On Friday in the morning we had sight of land at what are called the Ilheus Chãos.[27] These islets are five leagues beyond the Ilheu da Cruz.[28] From the bay of São Bras to the said Ilheu da Cruz it is 60 leagues, and as much from the Cape of Good Hope to the bay of São Bras;[29] from the Ilheus Chãos to the last padrão which Bartolomeu Dias placed[30] is another five leagues, and from the padrão to the Rio do Infante 15 leagues.[31]

On Saturday following we passed the last padrão. As we coasted along two men began to run along the beach opposite where we were going. This land is very charming and well settled; we saw many cattle wandering about on the land here; and the further we advanced the fairer did the land become, and the higher the groves of trees.

The following night we lay to, because we were as far advanced as the Rio do Infante, which was the last land that Bartolomeu Dias discovered. On the following day we continued along the coast with the wind astern until the time of vespers, when the wind sprang round to the east and we tacked out to sea. So we proceeded, tacking alternately out to sea and to the land, until Tuesday, about sunset, when the wind again turned to the west. We accordingly lay to that night, so that the next day we might recognize the land or find where we were.[32] As soon as morning came we went straight towards the land; and at 10 o'clock that day we found ourselves level with the Ilheu da Cruz, which was 60 leagues astern of where we reckoned to be: this was caused by the currents, which are very strong here.[33]

This same day we returned to the course that we had already run, with a very strong stern wind which lasted three or four days and we overcame the currents which we had feared would not let us achieve what we desired. From that day onwards it pleased God in His mercy for us to go forward and not astern; and may it please Him that it will be so always.

On Christmas day, which was the 25th day of the month of December, we had discovered 70 leagues of coast.[34] On this day, after we had dined, while setting a bonnet, we found the mast had a crack in it, a fathom below the yard, which opened and shut. We patched it up with shrouds, until we could make a sheltered port where we could repair it. On Thursday we anchored off the coast, where we took in much fish;[35] and when sunset approached we again set sail and followed our course. Here we lost an anchor in the sea, because a cable broke.

From here we went so far out to sea without touching port that we had scarcely any water to drink and our food had to be cooked in salt water. For drink they gave us only a quartilho[36] [a day]. It was accordingly essential to reach a port.

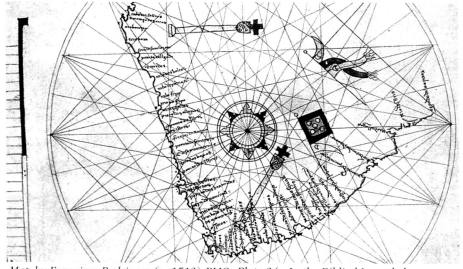

Map by Francisco Rodrigues (c. 1513), PMC, Plate 34. In the Bibliothèque de la Chambre des Députés, Paris. The earliest known map to show latitudes of South Africa, from Dias and his Successors, 1988, p. 107.

Vasco da Gama
The Diary of His Travels through African Waters 1497–1499

On Thursday which was the 10th day of January[37] we had sight of a small river, and here we anchored off the coast. The next day we went in the boats to the shore, where we found many black men and women. They were large in body; and among them was a Senhor. The Commander-in-Chief ordered one Martim Afonso, who had travelled in Manicongo for a very long time, to go ashore, and another man with him; and they were made warmly welcome. The Commander-in-Chief sent that Senhor a jacket, a cap, and a bracelet. He said that anything he had in his land that we needed he would give us with good will; and this the said Martim Afonso understood. That night the said Martim Afonso and the other man went with that Senhor to sleep in their houses, and we returned to our vessels. On the way that Senhor put on what they had given him and said with much satisfaction to those who came to meet him, 'Look what they gave me', and they clapped hands out of courtesy; and this they did three or four times until he reached the village, where he went about all over the place clothed as he was, until he went himself into a house, and he ordered the two men to be lodged. They went with him to a kraal, and there he ordered for them porridge of millet (of which there is much in that land) and a chicken like those of Portugal. All that night men and women came to see them. When it came to morning the Senhor went to see them and told them to return. He ordered two other men to go with them, and he gave them chickens for the Commander-in-Chief, saying that he would show what they had given him to a great Senhor whom they had, who seems to us to be the king of that land; and when they reached the port where the boats were there came with them a good 200 men who had come to see them.

This land, it seemed to us, is densely populated. There are in it many Senhores. The women seemed to be more numerous than men, because wherever there came 20 men there came 40 women. The houses of this land are of straw. The arms of these people are very large bows[38] and arrows, and assagais of iron. In this land there seemed to be much copper, which they wore on their legs and arms and in their kinky hair. Equally, in this land, is also tin, which they use on the hilts of daggers, the sheaths of which are of iron. The people of this land greatly prize linen cloth, and they gave us much of this copper for as many shirts as we cared to give. These people carry some large calabashes of salt water from the sea inland, and pour it into pits in the ground and make salt from it.

We were five days here taking in water, which those coming to see us carried to the boats, but we did not take in all the water we wanted to because the wind favoured the voyage, and we were anchored off the coast in the ocean rollers. To this land we gave the name Terra da Boa Gente,[39] and to the river, the Rio de Cobre.

One Monday, continuing by sea, we had sight of a very low land and of some groves of trees, some of which were very high and close together. Continuing on this route,[40] we saw the broad mouth of a river. Because it was necessary to know and identify where we were, we anchored. On Thursday, at night, we entered, the vessel *Berrio* being already there, having entered the previous day, which was the 8th day before the end of January. This land is very low and swampish; and in it are great groves of trees, which give many fruits of many kinds and the men of this land eat of them.

These people are black, and the men are of good physique; they go about naked except that they wear small pieces of cotton cloth with which they cover their genitals; and the Senhores of this land wear larger cloths. The young women in this land look good; they have their lips pierced in three places and there they wear some pieces of twisted tin. These people were at very much ease with us, and brought out to us in the vessels what they had, in dugout canoes. And we similarly went to their village to take water.

After we had been here two or three days there came two Senhores of this land to see us; they were so haughty that they did not value anything that was given them. One of them was wearing a cap on his head with piping worked in silk, and the other was wearing a furry cap of green satin. There came in their company a youth who, we gathered from gestures, came from another far-off country and said that he had already seen great vessels like those that carried us. With these signs we rejoiced greatly, because it seemed to us we were going to reach where we wanted to go. These noblemen ordered huts to be made of branches on land alongside the river, opposite the vessels, in which they stayed for about seven days. Each day they sent to the vessels to trade cloths that bore marks of red ochre; and when they tired of being there they went up the river in their dug-out canoes.

We were 32 days in this river during which we took in water, careened the vessels, and repaired the mast of *Rafael.* Here many of our men fell ill, their feet and their hands swelling, and their gums growing so over their teeth that they could not eat. Here we placed a padrão to which they gave the name Padrão of São Rafael, from the name of the vessel that carried it. To the river they gave the name Rio dos Bons Sinais.[41]

We departed from here one Saturday, the 24th day of the month of February. That day we tacked out to sea, and the night following we sailed eastwards, to withdraw from the coast – which was very lovely to look at. On Sunday we made to the north-east, and when it came to the hour of vespers we saw three small islands out to sea, two of them with great groves of trees and the other bare and smaller than the others; and from one to the other would be four leagues.[42] Because it was night we put out on a seaward tack and we passed by them at night. On the next day we continued on our way, and proceeded for six days at sea, lying to at night. On Thursday, the 1st day of the month of March, in the afternoon, we had sight of the islands and land which I proceed to describe. Because it was late we put about on a seaward tack, and lay until morning. We then came to enter the following land.[43]

On Friday morning Nicolau Coelho, entering that bay, mistook the channel and found a shoal. While putting about towards the other vessels that followed astern of him he saw some boats under sail approaching him from that island, from the village, coming with great pleasure to welcome the Commander-in-Chief and his brother. As for ourselves, we stopped going on that seaward tack in order to anchor. The further we advanced the more they followed us, signalling to us to wait for them. After we had anchored in the lagoon of that island whence had come the boats, seven or eight of those boats and dug-out canoes reached us, the men playing some trumpets that they carried, and telling us to proceed within, and that if we wished they would pilot us into port. They entered into our vessels, and ate and drank just what we were eating. After they were satisfied they departed.

The captains in counsel decided that we should enter this bay, so that they would know the trade of these people; and that Nicolau Coelho should go first with his vessel to sound the bar, and that if he could enter then they would enter. As Nicolau Coelho went to enter he struck on the point of that island and broke the rudder. As soon as he struck he went out into deep water; and I was with him there. As soon as we gained the deep water we struck our sails and cast the anchors two crossbow-shots from the village.[44]

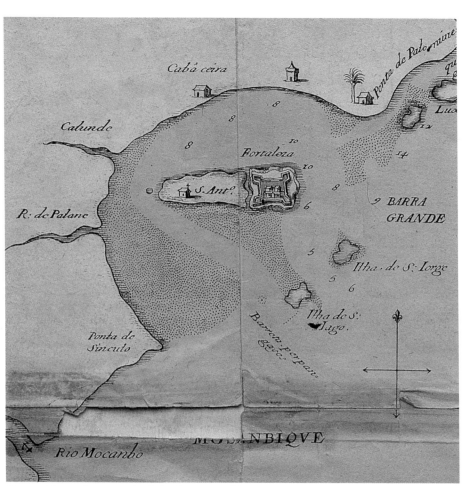

Moçambique, from map by João Teixeira, 1649.

The men of this land are ruddy in colour and of good physique. They are of the Mohammedan faith, and they speak like Moors.[45] Their clothes are of very thin linen and cotton, of many-colours and stripes; they are rich and embroidered. They all wear toques on their heads with piping of silk worked with gold thread. They are merchants, and they trade with white Moors, four of whose vessels were here at this place, carrying gold and silver, cloves, pepper and ginger, rings of silver with many pearls, and seed-pearls and rubies and the like. Men of this land wear all these things.

It seemed to us from what they said that all these things were transported here, and that the Moors brought them, except the gold; and that further on, where we were going, there was much, and the stones, seed-pearls and spices were in such quantity that it was not necessary to trade for them, but simply to collect them in baskets. All this a seaman understood who had been a captive of the Moors, and for this reason understood those whom we found here. Further, declared the said Moors we met, on the route we were following we would find many shoals; we would also find many cities along the coast; and we would have to call at an island on which half the population were Moors and half Christians; the Christians were always waging war on the Moors; and this island had much wealth.

Further, they told us that Prester John was situated close to there and that he had many cities on the sea-coast; the inhabitants of them were great merchants and had great ships; but Prester John was situated a great distance inland, and it was not possible to travel there except on camels. Those Moors brought here two Indian Christian captives. These things, and many others, these Moors told us, which made us so happy that we shouted with joy; and we begged God to grant us health so that we should see what we all desired.

In this town and island which they call Mocobiquy [Moçambique] was a Senhor they called Sultan, who was like Viceroy; he frequently came to our vessel accompanied by attendants. The Captain used to feed him very well, and gave him a present of hats, short hooded cloaks, and coral necklaces. He was so upset that he scorned whatever they gave him, and he asked that they should give him scarlet cloth, but we did not carry any; but of what we had, we gave him. The Commander-in-Chief one day gave him a banquet, at which were many figs and conserves, and asked him to give two pilots to go with us. He agreed to this, on condition that we satisfied them. The Commander-in-Chief gave to each 30 meticals of gold[46] and two hooded cloaks, on condition that from that day when they should receive this, if they wished to disembark, one of them should remain always in the vessel. They were very content with this.

On Saturday, the 10th day of the month of March, we departed, but came to anchor a league out to sea, close to an island, so that on the Sunday we might hear mass, and those who wished might go to confession and to communion.

One of those pilots remained on the island, and after anchoring we armed two boats for we had to go for him. In one went the Commander-in-Chief, and in the other Nicolau Coelho. As they set out there came against them five or six boats with many people carrying their bows with very long arrows, and shields, summoning them to return to the village. The Commander-in-Chief, when he saw this, seized the pilot he carried with him and ordered that they should fire the bombards against those who came in the boats. Paulo da Gama who was remaining on the vessels so that in case of need they might go to aid, as soon as he heard the bombards made all sail on the vessel *Berrio*, and the Moors, already fleeing, as soon as they saw the vessel under sail, fled still faster and reached land before the *Berrio* could reach them. And so we returned to our anchorage.

On Sunday we heard our mass on the island in a grove of high trees. After mass we returned to the ships, and at once made sail, and followed on our way, with many chickens and pigeons, traded here for some small yellow glass beads.

The ships of this land are large and without decks. They are not nailed, and sail tightly bound with esparto cord; and their boats the same. Their sails are of palm matting, and their mariners have Genoese needles by which to steer, and quadrants and sea-charts.[47] The palm trees of this land yield fruit as large as melons and the pulp inside is what they eat, and it tastes of sedgy hazelnut. There are also cucumbers, and many melons, which they brought us to barter. On that day when Nicolau Coelho entered, the Senhor of this land came to the vessel with many people, and he entertained him very well and gave him a red cowl. The Senhor gave him some black prayer beads as a pledge, and asked Nicolau Coelho for the boat, to go in it, and this he gave him. After he was on land and took with him to his house those who went with him, and he invited them in. Later he ordered them to go, and sent Nicolau Coelho a jar of crushed dates made into a preserve with cloves and cumin. Later he sent also to the Commander-in-Chief many things. This he did while it seemed to him that we were Turks or Moors from some other part, for he asked if we came from Turkey, and that we should show him the bows of our country and the books of our law. After they knew that we were Christians they ordered us to be taken and killed by treachery, but the pilot whom we were carrying with us revealed everything they were ordering to be done against us, if this could be put into action.

Life on board. Sketch by Roque Gameira, História da Colonização Portuguesa do Brasil, *II, p. 51.*

On Tuesday we sighted a land with [high hills] beyond a point, which point has along the shore a grove of high trees like elms and not densely spread. This land would be at most 20 leagues from the place we had left.[48] Here we lay becalmed on Tuesday and Wednesday. The night following we went on a tack from the sea in a very light wind. When it came to morning we found ourselves four leagues astern of Moçambique. That day we sailed until evening when we anchored close to the island where they said mass the previous Sunday; and there we were for eight days waiting on the weather.

During this time the king of Moçambique sent to tell us he wished to make peace with us and to be our friend. For this peace he sent as ambassador a white Moor who was a shareef, that is to say a cleric, who was a great drunkard. While we were here a Moor came aboard one of our vessels with a boy, his son, saying he wished to go with us because he had come from close to Mecca; he had come to Moçambique as pilot of a ship of this land.

Because the weather did not aid us, it was necessary to enter the port of Moçambique to take in water. This watering place was on the mainland. Those of the island drink of this water, for they have nothing else but salt water. One Thursday we entered the said port and as it was night we launched the boats. At midnight the Commander-in-Chief and Nicolau Coelho and some others of us went to see where the water was. We took with us the Moorish pilot who was more interested in fleeing if he could than in showing us where the water was; and he carried on in such a way that he did not show us where it was; or else he did not wish to do so. We wandered about in this way until dawn, and then we returned to the vessels.

When it came to evening we went there again with the same pilot. When we were close to the watering place about 20 of them moved along the beach, skirmishing with assagais in their hands, and it seemed to us that they were going to defend the water. The Commander-in-Chief ordered three bombard shots to be fired to give us space to leap ashore. As soon as we were out of the boats they hid themselves in the bush, and we took in as much water as we wanted. When we returned it was about sundown. We found that a negro of pilot João de Coimbra had fled.

On Saturday, the 24th day of the month of March, the eve of the day of our Lady, in the morning, a Moor came straight out to the vessels to say that if we wished for water then we should go get it, giving us to understand that there was something there that would cause us to turn back. The Commander-in-Chief, as soon as he saw this, determined that we should go there to show them we could do them harm if we wished to. Accordingly, with the boats armed, and bombards in their sterns, we at once went to the village. The Moors had made very adequate palisades, fences sufficiently together in such a way that we were not able to see those who were behind it. They were moving about along the shore, armed with little shields, assagais, scimitars and bows, and slings with which they hurled stones at us. But we kept them such company with the bombards that they found it convenient to leave the beach and place themselves behind the palisade that they had made; but this caused them more damage than profit. We were engaged on this for about three hours; and we saw two men killed there, one of whom we killed on the beach and the other within the stockade. After we became tired of doing this we returned to the vessels to dine. At once they began to flee, and to load their belongings into dugout canoes to carry them to a village that is on the other side.

After we had dined we went in the boats to try and take some of them, to exchange for the two Indian Christians that they had taken captive, and the negro who had run away. For this purpose we pursued a dug-out canoe of the shereef, which was loaded with goods, and another that was carrying four negroes. Paulo da Gama took the latter, and that which was loaded with goods was deserted by those who were in it as soon as it reached the land and it was left on the shore. We took this and others that we found on the shore. The negroes that we took there we carried to the vessels. In the canoes we found many cloths of fine cotton and palm baskets, a large earthen vessel of butter, glass bowls of waters, books of their law, a chest with many skeins of cotton, a net also of cotton, and many wicker baskets full of millet. The Commander-in-Chief gave all those things taken there to the seamen who found them in company with himself and the other captains, except the books which he kept to show the King.

On Sunday following we went and took in water. On Monday we went in front of the village with the boats armed, and the Moors spoke from behind the houses because they did not dare come on to the beach. After firing bombard shots at them we returned to the vessels. On Tuesday we left from in front of the village and anchored close to the islets of São Jorge, where we were for three days yet, hoping that God would give us favourable weather.

On Thursday, the 29th day of the said month, we departed from the said islets. Because the wind was light, when it came to Saturday morning which was the 31st of the said month, we were 28 leagues from the said islets. On the said day, in the morning, we were as far advanced as the land of Moors: we had been driven back by the currents, which were strong.[49]

On Sunday, the 1st day of the month of April, we were up to some islands which were close to the mainland. To the first of these said islands they gave the name Açoutado, because on the Saturday, in the afternoon, the Moorish pilot we were taking with us, lied to the Captain, telling him that these islands were part of the mainland, and because of this he was ordered to be flogged. The ships of this land navigate between the mainland and these islands, and go in four fathoms, and we went to sea of them. These islands are numerous and many close together, so that we could not distinguish some from others; and they are populated. On the Monday we had sight of other islands, which are five leagues out to sea.[50]

On Wednesday, which was the 4th day of April, we set the sails and went to the north-west, and before midday had sight of a fruitful land and two islands close to it; and this land has around it many shoals. As soon as we were close to it the pilots recognized it and said that the island of the Christians was astern of us three leagues. We laboured all day to see if we could cover this distance, but because of the strong westerly wind we could not.[51] Then the captains took counsel, that we should make for a city which was four days journey from us; which city is called Mōbaça [Mombasa].

This island[52] was one we wanted to come to, for the pilots we brought with us said that it was of Christians. We made for it, already late, with a very strong wind. Near nightfall we saw a very large island situated to the north,[53] which island the Moorish pilots we were carrying with us, told us, had one village of Christians, another of Moors.

This night following we tacked out to sea, and when it came to morning we did not see land. We then made way to the north-by-west, and when evening came we saw land.

This night following we made way to the north-by-west, and in the dawn watch to the north-north-west. Going with the wind holding, two hours before first light the vessel S. Rafael ran aground, on shallows two leagues from the mainland. As soon as she struck shouts warned the others who were coming astern, and as soon as they heard the shouts they anchored, a bombard-shot away, and they launched boats. At low tide the vessel came to rest on dry land. With boats they launched many anchors into the sea, and when it came to the tide of the day, which was high water, the vessel came off, at which all greatly rejoiced. On the mainland, to the right of the shoals, is a mountain range, very high and lovely, to which they gave the name Serras of São Rafael and the shoals the same.[54]

While the vessel was aground, two dug-out canoes came up to it and to us, which brought many oranges, sweet and very good, and better than those of Portugal. There remained on the vessel two Moors who the next day went with us to a city, which is called Mombasa.

On the Saturday, on the morning of the 7th day of the said month, the eve of Palm Sunday, we went along the coast and saw some islands out to sea, 15 leagues from the mainland, and extending six leagues in length, on which islands are many masts with which they mast the ships of the land. They are all inhabited by Moors.[55]

At sunset we anchored in front of the said city of Mombasa and we did not enter the port. When we arrived there came to us a zavra[56] loaded with Moors, and in front of the city were many ships, all beflagged with their standards. We, to keep them company, did the same, and more, to our vessels, for we lacked nothing except people, for already the few we had were very ill. There we anchored with much pleasure, it seeming to us that we could go the next day to hear mass on land with the Christians who, they told us, were here, separate from the Moors; and they had their own alcaide.

The pilots whom we were carrying said that on this island of Mombasa were Moors and Christians; they lived apart one from the other; each had its own Senhor; and as we had arrived here they would receive us with much honour and take us to their houses. This was said by them because of what they desired to do, and it was not to be.

That night following, at midnight, there came in a zavra about 100 men, all with short broad-swords and small round shields. As they came to where the Commander-in-Chief was, they wanted to board with their arms and this he did not wish. There did not enter more that four or five, of the most respectable of them. They were about two hours with us, and then they went. It seemed to us that this visit was to see if they could seize some of these vessels.

On Palm Sunday[57] the king of Mombasa sent the Commander-in-Chief a sheep, many oranges and citrons,[58] and sugar-canes. He sent also a ring as security, and sent that if we wanted to enter [the port] he would give him everything that he might need. And there came two men, very white, who said that they were Christians – and to us it seemed so too – with this present.

The Commander-in-Chief sent him [the king] a string of coral beads and the message that he would enter the next day. On this day there remained in the Captain's vessel four of the most respected Moors. The Captain sent two men to the king of this city further to confirm the peace. They, as soon as they landed, were accompanied by a crowd of people to the gate of the palace and before they could reach the king they passed through four doors, where there were four door-keepers, each at his door, with naked cutlass in hand. When they reached the king he made them very welcome, and ordered that they be shown the city. They went to a house of two Christian merchants; and they showed these two men a card which they venerated since it was a sketch of the Holy Ghost.[59]

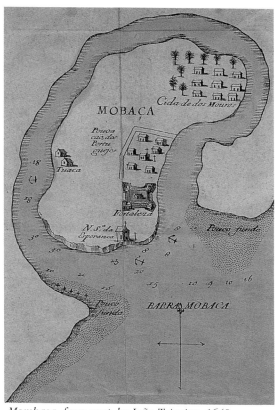

Mombasa, from map by João Teixeira, 1649.

After all this viewing the king sent samples of cloves, pepper and ginger, and three-month wheat, to the Captain, and these we could load.

On Tuesday, while raising anchors to go inside, the vessel of the Commander-in-Chief did not want to come round, and went astern. Then we turned to launch the anchors. In the vessels with us were Moors who, after they saw we were not leaving, retreated to a zavra; and going on to the poop the pilots who came from Moçambique with us threw themselves into the water, and those on the zavra took them in. When night came the Captain dropped boiling oil on the flesh of two Moors that we had brought with us from Moçambique to make them say if any treachery had been ordered. They said that as soon as we were inside they had orders to take us and avenge what we had done in Moçambique. When this was about to be done to the other he, with his hands tied, jumped into the sea; and the other threw himself in during the morning watch.

This night following, at midnight, there came two dug-out canoes with many men who threw themselves in to swim, while the canoes remained at a distance. Some went to the vessel *Berrio*, and the others came to the *Rafael*. Those who went to the *Berrio* began to chop the anchor-cable. Those on watch thought they were tunny fish, and identifying them shouted to the other vessels. Others were already grasping the chains and shrouds of the foremast of the *Rafael*. As soon as they were discovered they silently descended and fled. These dogs ordered these and many other wickednesses, but our Lord did not want them to succeed because they did not believe in Him.

This city is large, set on high ground beaten by the sea; and it is a port entered every day by many vessels. It has at its entrance a padrão;[60] and it has a small town close to the sea, and a fortress below. Those who went on land told us that they saw walking through the town many men who were prisoners with irons on them, and these it seems to us must have been Christians, for the Christians in this land are at war with the Moors.

The Christians who are in this city are as temporary traders, very subjected, for they can do nothing beyond what the Moorish king orders. It pleased God, in His mercy, that as soon as we were close to this city at once all the ill that we brought with us became healthy, for this land has very good airs. We were still here on Wednesday and Thursday,[61] even after we had learnt of the malice and treachery which those dogs wanted to do against us. We left that morning, with little wind, and anchored about eight leagues from Mombasa, close to land.

About break of day we saw two boats to leeward of us, out to sea, about three leagues away. We at once made for them, to take them, for we desired to have pilots who could take us to where we desired to go. When it came to the time of vespers we were up to one of the said boats and we took it; and the other two found shelter on land. In that which we took we found 17 men, and gold and silver, and much millet and provisions, and a young woman, wife of an old man, an honourable Moor, who was there. As soon as we arrived close to them they all threw themselves into the sea, and we went taking them with our boats.

On this same day, at sunset, we dropped anchor directly in front of a place which is called Mjlindes [Malindi] which is 30 leagues from Mombasa; and from Mombasa to this town of Malindi are the places which follow: chiefly Benapa and Toça and Nùguo Qujonte.[62]

On Easter day[63] the Moors we had taken captive told us that in the said town of Malindi were four vessels of Christians, who were Indians, and if we should like to convey them there would give us, for themselves, Christian pilots, and everything else we might need, including meats, water, wood and other things. The Commander-in-Chief, who greatly desired to have pilots of that land, treated on this matter with the Moors, and we dropped anchor in front of that town, half a league from land. Those of the town did not dare to come out to the vessels for they had been already informed, and knew that we had taken a boat with the Moors.

On Monday morning the Commander-in-Chief placed that old Moor on a shoal in front of the town, and a dug-out canoe came for him. The said Moor went to tell the king what the Captain wanted, and how he would be happy to make peace with him. After dinner the Moor came in a zavra, in which the king of that town had sent one of his cavaliers and a shereef and three sheep. He also sent to say to the Captain that he would rejoice to have peace between them, which would be advantageous; and if there was anything in his land that he wanted, he would give it to him happily, including the pilots. The Commander-in-Chief sent word that he would enter the port the next day. He sent at once by the messengers a balandrau, two strings of coral beads, three basins, a hat, a rattle, and two lambels.[64]

Betimes on Tuesday we approached closer to the town, and the king sent the Captain six sheep, and many cloves and much cumin, ginger, nutmeg and pepper, and a message to say that he would like to meet him at sea: he would go in his zavra, and the Captain could go in his boat.

On Wednesday after dinner the king came in a zavra close to the vessels; and the Captain went out in his boat, which had been well prepared. When he arrived where the king was, the said king and he lay alongside, and they exchanged many good words. Among these, the king invited the Captain to go with him to his house to be at ease, and he would then enter the Captain's vessels. The Captain told him that he did not have permission from his Senhor to go on land and that if he did go on land a bad report would be given to him who had sent him there. The king replied that if *he* were to go to the vessels, what account could *he* give to his people, and what would they say? He asked if he could have the name of our king and he asked that this be written down; and he said that when we returned he would send an ambassador, or write to him.

After they had talked, each one as much as he wanted to, the Captain ordered that all the Moors whom we had taken prisoner be given him, which made him very content; and he said that this made him happier than if he had been given a town.

The king, at ease, made a circuit of the vessels, where many bombards were fired for him, and he greatly enjoyed seeing the firing. They passed about three hours in this. When he went he left a son of his in the vessel, and a shereef; and there went with him to his house two of our men whom he had invited to see his residences. Further he said to the Captain that since he did not want to land the next day he would walk along the shore, and order his cavaliers to ride their horses.

These are things the king wore and brought: firstly, a robe of damask lined with green satin, and a toque on his head, very rich; two bronze chairs with their cushions, and a canopy of crimson satin, round and hanging from a beam. And he brought an old man as attendant, who carried a short broadsword with a silver scabbard. And he brought many Moorish trumpets, and two ivory tusks the height of a man, with many carvings, played through a hole in the middle. And the horns harmonized very well with the trumpets.

On Thursday the Commander-in-Chief and Nicolau Coelho went in boats with bombards in their sterns past the town. On the shore were many men moving about and among them two men on horseback were sham-fighting, causing much amusement by their display. Then they took the king from a stone staircase of his palace in a palanquin to the boat where the Captain was. There he begged the Captain to go on land, because he had a father who was crippled and would love to see him; and he and his children would go in his vessels [as hostages]. The Captain excused himself.

Here we found four ships of Christians of India. The first time they came to the vessel of Paulo da Gama, where the Commander-in-Chief was. There they were shown a decorated panel on which was Our Lady with Jesus Christ in her arms, at the foot of the cross, and the apostles. The Indians, when they saw this retable, threw themselves on the ground; and while we were there, they came to say their prayers, and brought cloves and pepper, and other things which they dedicated.[65]

These Indians are swarthy men. They wear few clothes. They wear great beards, and the hairs of the head are very long and plaited. They do not eat bovine meat according to what they say. And their language is different from that of the Moors; some of them know a little Arabic from continuous communication they have with them.

On that day when the Commander-in-Chief went out in boats to the town, the ships of the Christian Indians fired many bombards, and raised their hands whenever they passed, crying out with much joy, Christe! Christe![66] This day they begged permission of the king to let them make a night festa for us. And when night came they made a great festa, and fired many bombards and let off rockets and gave great shouts. These Indians further told the Commander-in-Chief that he should not go ashore: he should not trust musical diversions because they did not stem from either heart or will.

On the following Sunday, which was the 22nd day of the month of April, there came a zavra of the king. On board was an intimate friend of the king. Since for two days they had not come to the vessels the Captain seized him, and insisted that the king send him the pilots he had promised. When he received this message the king sent at once a Christian pilot and the Captain let that nobleman go. And we liked very much the Christian pilot that the king sent us.[67]

Here we learnt that the island which they told us about in Moçambique was of Christians, is under the same king as Moçambique, and half of it is of Moors and half of Christians. And this island has many seed pearls. The name of the island is Quylvee [Kilwa]. It was to here that the Moorish pilots wanted to take us, and we desired to see, for it seemed to us that it was as they said.

This town of Malindi is situated on a bay, along a beach. This town looks like Alcochete.[68] The houses are tall and very well whitewashed, and have many windows. Along the town on the land side, close to the houses, is a very large grove of palm-trees; and on all the land around are fields of millet and other vegetables.

We were there in front of this town for nine days,[69] and in those nine days were festas, many sham-fights on foot, and many musical concerts.

On Wednesday, the 26th day of the said month [April], we departed from here, with the pilot the king gave us, for a city which is called Qualicut [Calicut], of which city the king had information.[70] We went eastwards towards it. Here the coast runs north and south, for the mainland makes a great bay and strait; in which bay, we were informed, are many cities of Christians and Moors, and a city which is called Cambaia and 600 known islands; here also is the Red Sea, and the House of Mecca.[71] On the Sunday we had sight of the North Star, which we had not seen for a long time. On Friday, the 18th[72] day of May, we saw a high land. For 23 days we had not seen land, going always on these days with the wind astern, which made possible this crossing of at least 600 leagues.[73]

[On 20 May, Vasco da Gama reached India and anchored off Calicut.][74]

We sailed for so long on this [return] crossing that we took three months less three days on it,[75] there were so many calms and contrary winds experienced on it in such a way that all the people fell ill, with their gums swelling over their teeth in such a way that they could not eat; in the same

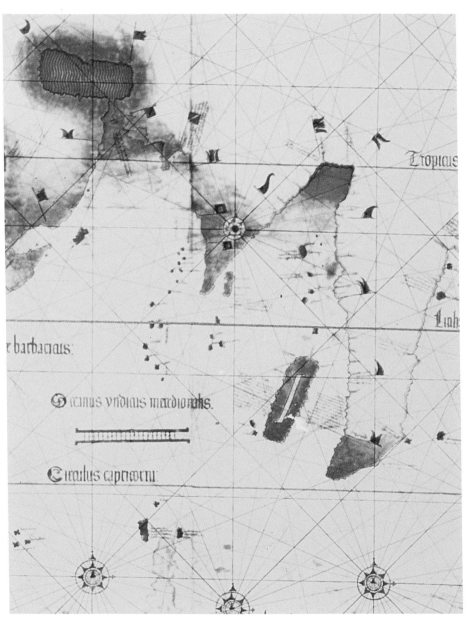

Close up of the Cantino map depicting India and the Arabian Sea. Biblioteca Estense Universitaria, Modena.

way their legs swelled up and there were other swellings on the body, and they worked on a man so that he could die without any other illness. From this there died in the said time 30 men, apart from as many others who had already died. Those who could manage each ship were seven or eight; and these were not as healthy as they should have been; from this I affirm that if the crossing of that sea had lasted another 15 days there would have been nobody to sail the vessels. To such a point did we come we all became resigned to our fate. Sailing thus in such misfortune we made many promises to Saints, and petitions, from the vessels. The captains had already taken counsel that if the wind did not change for the better we should return to the land of India which we had left, and land there.

It pleased God in His mercy to grant such a wind that in about six days we reached land; at which we rejoiced as much as if we had seen Portugal, for we were hoping, with the help of God, to return there again. It was Wednesday, the 2nd day of January,[76] of year 1499. Because we were already close to land and it was night-time we turned about and anchored. When it was morning we sought the land, to know where our Lord had thrown us, for we did not now have with us a pilot or any other man who could calculate the ship's position, except that some said that we could only be among some islands that were before Moçambique, about 300 leagues of coast. This was because a Moor that we had taken at Moçambique, said the islands were very unhealthy and even those who lived on them suffered from our illnesses.

We found ourselves in front of a very great city with rows of several storeyed houses and in the middle of the city some large palaces and around the city were four towers. This city faced the sea. The Moors call it Mogadoxo [Mogadishu].[77] When we were sufficiently close to it we fired many bombard shots.

We made our way with a good stern wind along the coast, sailing by day and lying to by night, because we did not know how far we were from Malindi, which was where we wanted to go. On Saturday, which was the 5th day of the said month [January], in sultry heat, a thunderstorm suddenly struck, which broke the ties of the *Rafael*. While we were making repairs to the said vessel there came out to us from a small town called Pate[78] a privateer with eight boats and many people towards us, and when they came within bombard range we fired at them and they fled at once to land; we did not go after them because we did not have wind.

On Monday, which was the 7th day of the said month, we went and
anchored in front of Malindi where the king at once sent a long-boat which
brought many people, and he sent sheep. He sent to tell the captain that
he was very welcome. And for days he had been expecting him. And he
sent many other expressions of friendship and peace. The Captain sent
with those who came a man to land, to bring the next day the oranges
greatly desired by those ill we carried. These were brought at once, with
many other fruits; but they did not profit the ill, for the land affected them
in such a way that many died here. Many Moors came on board and by
order of the king brought many chickens and eggs to trade.

The captain, seeing that he had been done such honour at a time it was so
necessary for us, asked him for a service; he sent by one of our men who
knew how to speak Arabic, a message that he would like the king to give
a tusk of ivory which he could take to the King his Senhor, and he would
send him a padrão to place on land to remain as a sign of friendship.

The king said that he was very happy to do all that he had been asked
to do, from the love he had for the King of Portugal whom he wanted to
serve, and would be always at his service. At once he sent a tusk to the
captain and ordered the padrão to be brought to land.[79] And he sent a
Moorish youth to come with us, who wanted to come and see Portugal.
This Moor the king sent with strong recommendation to the captain; and
he further said that he sent the youth to the King of Portugal so that he
would know how much he desired his friendship. We were in this place
for five days, merry-making and recovering from so much labour we had
suffered in the crossing where all were on the verge of death.

On a Friday, in the morning, we left, and when it came to Saturday,
which was the 12th day of the said month, we passed close by Mombasa.
On Sunday we anchored on the shoals of São Rafael, where we put fire to
the vessel of this name because it was impossible to handle three vessels
with so few people. Here we passed all the goods of this vessel to the
two that remained to us. Here we were for 15 days, in front of a small
town called Taugata[80] from where they brought us many chickens for sale,
traded for shirts and bracelets.

One Sunday, which was the 27th day of the said month, we left from
here with a very good stern wind and the night following we lay-to.

Sketch by Roque Gameira of central nave, Jeronimos, Belem, História da Colonização Portuguesa do Brasil, *Vol. I, p. 11.*

When morning came we found ourselves close to a very large island which is called Jamgiber [Zanzibar], which is peopled by many Moors, which will be a good 10 leagues from the mainland.[81]

On the 1st day of February, in the afternoon, we anchored in front of the islands of São Jorge, in Moçambique. The next day, in the morning, we placed on the island where we had heard mass outward-bound, a padrão; and so heavy was a shower of rain that we were not able to make a fire to melt lead to set the cross; the padrão remained without it.[82] We made for the vessels and departed at once.

On the 3rd day of the month of March we arrived at the bay of São Bras, where we took much achoa[83] and many sea-wolves and penguins, which we salted for the sea; and on the 12th of the said month we departed. Beyond the watering place 10 or 12 leagues the wind blew from the west, in such a way that we turned to anchor in the said bay.

As soon as it was fair weather we returned on our way; and thanks to our Lord such good weather[84] prevailed that on the 20th day of the said month we passed the Cape of Good Hope. Those who reached here were in good health, but at times nearly died from the coldness of the strong breezes which we experienced here, which hit us all the harder and colder since we had come from such a hot area.[85]

We continued on our way, with great desire to arrive. We sailed with the wind astern which lasted for a good 27 days, in such a way that it placed us well in the approaches to the island of Santiago; on maritime charts the most that we could be from there was 100 leagues, and on some that we were already up to it. Here the wind fell; what there was was very little, and from ahead. To have knowledge of where we were, and with some thunderstorms that came to us from the land, we went from there as far as we could. On Thursday, the 25th day of the month of April, we found a depth of 35 fathoms; and all day we were on this route, and the least depth was 20 fathoms, and yet we were unable to have sight of land. The pilots said that we were on the shoals of the Rio Grande.[86]

(The diary ends.[87])

Notes

'Miles' in the notes are naturally nautical miles.

•1   At Restelo, some 4 miles down the Tagus from the port of Lisbon, was a fountain of fresh water, at which out-going vessels replenished supplies. In the mid 1400s a hermitage was built there, near high-water mark, dedicated to Santa Maria de Belem, St Mary of Bethlehem. In 1460 this hermitage, and adjoining properties within cross-bow shot, were donated by Prince Henrique to the Military Order of Christ, of which Henrique was master. The headquarters of the Order, at Tomar, provided friars to administer sacraments and baptise.

Barros described how on 'Saturday the 8th of July, as the hermitage was dedicated to our Lady and was a great place of pilgrimage, because of this devotion and to take leave of those who were going in the fleet, there came a great number of people. When Vasco da Gama was to embark, the friars of the hermitage with several priests who had come thither from the city to say mass arranged a devout procession in the following order: he and all his company went first with candles in their hands, and all the people of the city followed behind answering the litany which was chanted by the priests, until they came to the boats in which they were to embark. Here they all knelt in silence, and the vicar of the house made a general confession aloud, and afterwards absolved them ... During this ceremony such was the grief of all that the shore took possession of their tears ...' (Trans., GM Theal, *Records of South-Eastern Africa*, VI, Cape Town, 1900, p. 163.)

•2   See map.

•3   A Teixeira da Mota produced evidence that the league, towards the end of the 15th century, measured $16^2/_3$ to the degree (Congresso Internacional de História dos Descobrimentos, *Actas* II, Lisbon, 1961, pp. 299–307.) It was later evaluated at $17^1/_2$ to the degree, i.e. 3.4 miles, which was preferred by Leitão & Lopes, p. 321.

•4   These small-bore cannons threw stone balls, and were light enough to be mounted on a long-boat.

•5   The route would have been south-east. Two hundred leagues would have taken the vessels to approximately off Serra Leóa.

•6   The vessel lay to under 'traquete e papafigos'. The former was a square fore-sail. 'Papafigos were bottom sails on the fore-mast and main-mast' (Leitão & Lopes, p. 392).

•7   The Diário records not a word about the route taken or the weather experienced between 22 August and 27 October of this historic semi-circling of the South Atlantic. The original diary probably contained some such information (even if the diarist was not a mariner) but such information was probably censored out. João II had ensured complete secrecy about voyages of exploration, and Manuel would have continued the natural policy of secrecy to thwart possible intrusion by competition from Spain. The subject was treated by Damião Peres (*História dos Descobrimentos Portugueses*, Porto, 1943, pp. 312–343), and by Gago Coutinho.

The 'Cantino' map of 1502 referred to in the Introduction was a superb production by an unknown Portuguese cartographer. It was drawn on three sheets of parchment, pasted on cloth. It measured 2.20 metres in length. Of significance is an alteration in the delineation of Brazil. 'A piece of parchment was pasted over the north and north-eastern parts, covering the original drawing of the coastline, which was thus moved westwards; the direct study of the original, the prolongation added to the pole of the flag placed near *Cabo de Sam Jorge*, and the repetition of this name in cursive handwriting, clearly disclose that the coast, when first drawn, ran along the outer border of the piece of parchment later pasted over it. Beyond this cape, the drawings had only one other name, *porto seguro* (Pedro Alvares Cabral's landfall), followed by the inscription recording the discovery. (*Portvgaliae Monvmenta Cartographica*, Vol. I, Lisbon, 1960, p. 10.)

The 'Cantino' map was described in detail by Duarte Leite in (*História da Colonização Portuguesa do Brasil*, Vol. II, Porto, 1923, pp. 225–284), who argued that all the names dated to the Cabral expedition and the armada of 1501, but the present editor considers that the name of Cabo de Sam Jorge may date to pre-1500, and even to pre-1494.

The present editor, appreciating the determined character of João II, and his insistence on the Tordesilhas line of longitude, agrees with Gago Coutinho that Portuguese explorers had discovered north-east Brazil by 1494. Common prudence would have caused Vasco da Gama to anchor off the coast of Brazil, possibly in an already discovered bay, to ensure sufficiency of fresh water for a crossing of unknown duration to south Africa. 'The standard European water container ... was the stave-built wooden barrel. Such containers did not guarantee that the water remained fit to drink, whether the problem was impurities of the original source, or even ingress of salt and bilge water. Barrels leaked easily ...' (RA Barker, 'Of caravelas, tides and water', *Stvdia* 54/55, 1996, pp. 107–108.)

•8   There has been much (unsettled) argument as to whether the 800 referred to distance from Lisbon, Santiago, or the African coast.

•9 These were seals. The commonest seal in south-west African waters is the Cape fur-seal *(Arctocephalus pusillis)*. It ranges usually within 90 miles of the coast. The 'quaqua', the 'Quegalho' and 'Cagalho' of Leitão & Lopes was probably the southern blackbacked gull, *Larus dominicus*. It ranges usually within 50 miles of land.

•10 Numbers of members of the expedition would have been familiar with *Sargassom natans*, floating in the Gulf Stream and Sargasso Sea. Cape west coast waters are dominated by dense forests of kelp, especially *Ecklonia maxima*, growing up to 12 m in length and up to 2 miles from shore.

•11 A Portuguese fathom was approximately 1.76 m (Leitão & Lopes).

•12 It was customary for Portuguese explorers to christen prominent natural features with the name of the saint for that day appearing in the book of *Guias Nauticas*. The name of St Helena does not appear in the November tables. Dictionaries of saints list 11 St Helenas, but not one dated 7 or 8 November.

St Helena Bay is open only to the north-west, and in summer time, when the south-easter blows, its surface is smooth. At its western end it is protected by Stompneus Point. Stompneus Bay is further sheltered by drying reefs and rocks. This is where Vasco da Gama would have stepped ashore, three assessors (including the present editor) had no hesitation in deciding, and on 8 November 1979, a monument presented by the Portuguese government was ceremoniously unveiled there.

•13 The diarist omitted reference to the vessels' need for fresh water. Castanheda, who had read the diary, wrote: 'After the fleet had anchored Vasco da Gama ordered the bay to be circled to see if any river of sweet water entered into it, and none being found he ordered Nicolau Coelho to search further along the coast, and he found one four leagues away to which the name Santiago was given, and it provided the fleet with water' (p. 10).

São Tiago's day was 25 July. The river may have been named in honour of the Order of Santiago e Espada, of which Gama was a Cavaleiro.

The São Tiago was the present Great Berg River, at the mouth of which is the fishing town of Laaiplek. The mouth is 10.6 miles from Stompneus Bay. The river was obviously flowing strongly. In recent years farmers 30 kilometres up the river have lost trees on its banks owing to salt pollution, caused by upriver dams.

•14   The word in the diary is 'baço', which Michaelis translates as 'dark brown, copper-coloured'. They probably called themselves 'Quena'. See note 22.

•15   The ceitil was a copper coin 18 mm in diameter, weighing 2.33 g.

•16   The Portuguese 'limpar' means to clean, clear, etc. In this context the meaning may be stretched to include careening.

•17   Pero de Alenquer had been Dias's chief pilot. He must have landed at the Cape of Good Hope, with a terrestrial astrolabe, taken an accurate observation of the sun, and determined the latitude. He did the same at St Helena Bay. According to the chronicler Barros, he landed there with a wooden astrolabe three palms (22 cm) in diameter, mounted on three legs (*Asia de Joam de Barros ...*, I, Coimbra, 1930, p. 126). The distance between latitudes was 30 leagues, approximately 102 miles. The actual difference between Stompneus Bay, 32°42' S, and Cape Point, 34°51' S, is 98 minutes, 98 miles.

•18   After rounding Stompneus Point Pero de Alenquer would have taken the vessels westwards to clear rocky points and outlying reefs before being able to steer south-south-east.

•19   Correct for the final 5 miles before Cape Maclear, the westernmost point of the Cape of Good Hope.

•20   False Bay is 17 miles wide at its mouth, and it extends inland for 17 miles.

•21   Dias named the cape São Bras because he passed it on the day of that saint. The name was anglicised to St Blaize. Nederlanders named the bay Mosselbaai in 1601.

•22   The actual distance is about 180 miles, about 53 leagues. The inhabitants of Mossel Bay would have been similar to those of Dias's bay 'das Alagoas', the Plettenberg Bay of today. Here a Portuguese ship anchored in 1506. Aboard were a merchant from Bavaria, Springer by name, and Jacob Fugger, member of an Augsburg banking firm, a 'patron of the arts' who knew the renowned painter and wood engraver Hans Burgkmair. Springer wrote a description of the inhabitants of 'Allago', which has been translated into English by Andrew Smith and WE Pasche ('Balthasar Springer at the Cape (1506)', *Quarterly Bulletin of the South African Library*, March 1997, pp. 93–98):

> At 'the Cape of Good Hope there begins another country. ... the inhabitants ... are (consist of) a half wild (savage) people and when you come to them they will no doubt give (exchange) an ox or a sheep for a small bowl (bell?) or

knife. There are many animals and there is much fish in this country and for
this reason these people will not take any money. Everybody goes naked
except they cover the genitals with hides or sheaths of leather and bind (tie)
the penises of the young boys up. Otherwise it is a pleasant land with good
water and fragrant herbs; and there is so much sand that men and women
(can) virtually (only) walk evenly on broad leather slippers. Quite a few of
them also have animal hides hanging around them in a similar fashion as one
wears short coats (cloaks) in our countries. Many of them have also adorned
their hair with rubber and pitch and for (the) sake of refinement and
ornamentation have hung and fastened many valuable precious stones into it.
They have a fast strange peculiar language ...'
This description was given to Burgkmair, who produced a woodcut which was
published in 1509 (see page 27).

•23 Both Cāo and Dias ascended the lower reaches of the Congo River and visited
the King of Congo. He sent a chief back with Dias asking the Portuguese king
to ship to Congo priests, stonemasons and carpenters, farmers experienced in
husbandry and tilling, and women to teach the making of bread. A Portuguese
party guided by Pero de Alenquer reached the kingdom in 1491.

•24 Seal Island lies 3 miles from Cape St Blaize, at the head of the bay,
600 yards from the shore. The Cape fur-seal is the main inhabitant. Old bulls
reach a weight of 360 kg. The southern elephant seal *(Mirounge leonine)* and the
leopard seal *(Hydrurga lepto nyx)* are also to be seen at times.

•25 These flightless sea-birds were penguins (Spheniscidae). Mesquita Perestrelo
called them 'sotilicairos'.

•26 The present editor has searched on a number of occasions for fragments of the
padrāo, but with no success.

•27 These Flat Islands were the Bird Islands of today.

•28 The Islet of the Cross, in Algoa Bay, later became known, from French maps,
as St Croix. Dias may have raised a wooden cross on the islet. In 1988, on the
500th anniversary of the naming by Dias, it was officially renamed Santa Cruz.

•29 From the Cape of Good Hope, point to point, into Mossel Bay, is about
210 miles. From Mossel Bay, point to point, to Santa Cruz is about 200 miles.

•30   Dias's padrão, dedicated to St Gregory, was raised at False Islet, better known as Kwaaihoek, 50 miles east-north-east of Port Elizabeth. Accounts of the recovery of fragments by the present editor and his brother Charles appeared in *South-East Africa 1488–1530* (Longmans, 1940, pp. 172–181) and *Congo to Cape: Early Portuguese Explorers* (Faber, 1973, pp. 115–145).

Of the expected inscription only a few small fragments bearing lettering were found. The reason for this was explained by Vernon Forbes ('Colonel RJ Gordon at the Dias Cross, Kwaaihoek 1786', *Quarterly Bulletin of the South African Library*, Cape Town, September 1972, pp. 1–4). Gordon, commander of the Nederlands garrison at the Cape, parked his ox-wagon at the mouth of the Boknes River, and 'went E.N.E. along the shore that is sandy here, to a prominent green hill on which I found a shattered to pieces old monument. I collected the fragments together in order to take them in the wagon to the Cape'. No trace of them has been found in the Castle or its grounds. Additional information was provided by Patrick Cullinan, who found a copy of a letter written by Gordon after his return to the Cape, which included, 'On a hill jutting out into the sea – a ruined monument. From it I carried away three stones which are covered with inscriptions. On one side there are Roman letters ... and on the other side there are Arabic ones ... The stone is a kind of marble ... Some Hottentots have told me that the caffers who lived in these parts a while ago, but who are now living more to the east, believed that this monument served to make women fertile when they rubbed themselves against it.' (Ibid., December 1982, p. 169.)

•31   Fifteen leagues, at 3.4 miles to the league, 51 miles, would have taken the vessels to within one mile of the mouth of the Keiskama River. Included in Pacheco Pereira's work was a list of features and their latitudes: the Rio do Infante was in 33°15' S. The mouth of the Keiskama is in 33°21' S. Mesquita Perestrelo, who survived the wreck of the *São Bento* and surveyed the coast 1575–1576, declared that the scene of the wreck was at the Rio do Infante, at 33°15' S.

•32   Use of the word 'reconhecer', normally 'to recognise', suggests that there were members of the expedition who had sailed along that coast before. The Michaelis dictionary, however, gives more meanings to 'reconhecer', including '6. (mil.) to reconnoitre. 7. to observe, take a view of'.

•33   The Agulhas current was responsible. 'Between Durban and Port Elizabeth, the current takes the form of a relatively narrow (60–100 miles wide), deep and intense jet that hugs the continental slope and has a surface velocity varying generally between 2 and 4 knots. Because the continental shelf is narrow here, the western edge of the current is only a few miles off the coast.' (*South African Sailing Directions*, I, 1975, p. 32.)

•34   Where was Vasco da Gama on Christmas Day? Was he off Durban – or off Port St Johns? See Appendix 1.

•35   It is impossible to estimate the position of this fishing ground in the absence of information about the wind during these three days after Christmas. It was certainly not off the Durban Bluff as has been claimed by some. The Ponta da Pescaria which appeared in charts later in the 16th century was, according to Perestrelo, in latitude $29^{1}/_{3}°$ S, i.e. near the mouth of the Tugela River.

•36   A quartilho was 0.35 litre.

•37   10 January was actually a Wednesday; either the day of the week was wrong, or the date. There are numerous similar discrepancies in the manuscript.

•38   An Indo-Portuguese sketch of about 1540 shows a dark figure drawing a bow, (wrongly) entitled 'cafre do cabo esperança'. (Comission of Portugal for the Seville Universal Exhibition 1992, *Portugal and the Discoveries*, p. 106.)

•39   The 'small river' was the Inharrime. This flows into Lake Poelala, inland from Zavora Point, and then for some 40 miles passes through a series of lagoons, close and parallel to the coast. It eventually issues into the sea, at Aguada de Boa Paz, in latitude 24°53' S. This area was the Terra da Boa Gente, the Land of the Good People.

•40   The distance from the mouth of the Inharrime River to the mouth of the Quelimane, the next harbour entered, is 570 miles, coasting. Sailing direct from Cape Bazaruto to the Quelimane, keeping east of the Sofala bank, the distance is 60 miles shorter, and the route safer. Gama was obviously determined to keep clear of Sofala – with advice perhaps, from a previous Portuguese expedition. Pacheco Pereira in his *Esmeraldo* wrote (Kimble, p. 4) that Manuel's 'captains discovered anew [novamente] the great mine which some hold to be that of Ophir and is now called Çofala'.

•41   The river was the Quelimane, its mouth in latitude 18°15' S. The present editor searched for this padrão in 1951. He had the good fortune to meet Lieut. (later Vice-Admiral and President of the Sociedade de Geografia de Lisboa) JA Barahona Fernandes who was making a new survey of that section of the coast. He had found that the coastline was experiencing heavy maritime erosion – 1 km had disappeared in the previous 30 years: the site of the padrão was now a very considerable distance out to sea.

•42   These were the Ilhas Primeiras. Fogo Island in the 20th century had a few trees about 65 feet high. Crown Island was about 4 miles north-east. Casuarina Island, in latitude 17°06' S, lay 10 miles north-east of Crown and was 'covered with high casuarina trees and can be recognised at a considerable distance'. 'The Primeira islands and shoals lie on the outer edge of a coral bank fronting this part of the coast at distances varying from 23 to 5 miles.' (*Africa Pilot* III, pp. 225–226.) It is not known what prompted Vasco da Gama to name the islands Primeiras, the name which appears on the Cantino map.

•43   In the manuscript a blank space follows, which could have accommodated about 14 lines of writing.

•44   Moçambique Island, 1½ miles long, in latitude 15°02' S, lies in a wide bay which is partly sheltered by two islets 3 miles to seaward which Vasco da Gama named São Jorge. By 1538 the southern islet was called São Tiago. Nineteenth-century charts showed São Jorge as Ilha de Goa, and the southern one as Ilha de Sena.

•45   The 'Moors' were 'Arabs'.

•46   A metical (the spelling in the document), mitical, mithqal, was discussed by V Magalhães Godinho who concluded that at Sofala and Kilwa it was probably of the classical weight in Muslim countries, 4.25 grams. (*Os Descobrimentos e a Economia Mundial*, 1963, p. 213.)

•47   'The Arab Indian Ocean compass card … is well-known to most historians of navigation and consists of north and south points with 15 equal divisions between named after 15 prominent stars which rise and set approximately in the 15 directions … The most important of all the techniques used by the Arab sailors was that of measuring their latitude by means of stellar altitudes.' The 'quadrant' was 'an instrument consisting of nine tablets each with a string through it or with one string through them all. The nine tablets each had a different width to correspond with different angular altitudes on the horizon'. (GR Tibbetts, *The navigational theory of the arabs in the fifteenth and sixteenth centuries*, Agrupamento de Estudos Cartografia Antiga (AECA), Vol. XXXVI, Coimbra, 1969, pp. 8, 9.)

•48   The document has 'estes montes', 'these hills', but there has been no previous reference to hills. The copyist obviously made a slip, and Portuguese scholars have suggested it should read 'altos', 'high'. If the vessels had covered 20 leagues, about 68 miles, there would have been sight of Mount Sorisa, 70 miles north of Moçambique. 'The Sorisa range, several craggy peaks having the appearance of the ruins of some great city, rises abruptly from this level land, the peaks assuming every variety of form of sugar-leaf, cone, and round or square-topped pillars, in some cases seeming to overhang their bases. Mount Pillar, the highest and most remarkable of these, is a cone with a pyramidal-formed point, always appearing the same from all directions.' (*Africa Pilot* III, p. 250.)

•49 'From Cape Delgado to the equator, in February and March, although during the time of the N.E. monsoon, the winds are between E.N.E. and E.S.E.' 'A south-going current is usually experienced off Mozambique, its limits extending from near the outer reefs of that place to from 50 to 80 miles from the land; the velocity, which is at its maximum during the strength of the N.E. monsoon, and *vice versa*, varies from 2 to 4 knots.' (*Africa Pilot* III, pp. 32, 241.)

•50 These were the Kerimba islands. 'Kizeeva island is low with some slight undulations and is covered with scrub. Fumo island, standing on the northern end of the same reef, is the highest of all the Kerimba islands and is covered with thick, green, scrub. The Kerimba chain of islands, of which Kizeeva, just mentioned, is the southernmost, form an archipelago extending from Arimba head to Cape Delgado, a distance of 117 miles. In this space, the outer reefs and islands extend in some places as much as 13 miles from the mainland, and in most parts more than 10 miles ... The islands, generally low, well wooded and easily seen from seaward, have in some cases, a diversified surface of hill and dale, whilst many are mere coral islets, and the eighteen or nineteen openings, between the outer islands and reefs, lead into a still greater number of secure ports or convenient anchorages for small craft.' (*Africa Pilot* III, p. 255.)

•51 The island was Quiloa, Kilwa. Kilwa had been a state for 550 years before the first Europeans arrived. Covilhã's report to King João II would have stressed its importance as the most powerful and prosperous authority on the east coast of Africa. The sultan of Kilwa was paramount on the coast. Traders south-bound had to pay him duty, and north-bound a tax on gold from Sofala. The town, on the north-west side of the island, facing the harbour (in latitude 8°57' S), had impressive several-storeyed buildings, and a really Great Mosque, which reminded a later caller of the mosque at Cordoba. The captains would have known of Kilwa's strategic and mercantile importance and must have been infuriated by the failure of the pilots to recognise the approaches to the islands. The inability to beat back to it is however explainable: 'Kilwa island ... Current – Caution. The current is continuously north-going off all this part of the coast, and frequently sets in towards the land: it is strongest and most regular during the Southern monsoon, when its strength increases at times to 4 knots.' (*Africa Pilot* III, p. 287.)

•52 Mombasa.

•53 Mafia Island, 48 kilometres long.

•54 The range was the Usambara and a nearby town Taugata. 'Mtangata Reef,
which dries, extends about 2 miles eastward of Kas Mtangata. Mtangata Bay lies
between Mtangata Reef and Ras Kisangani' which is in latitude 5°11' S. Tanga Bay
lay to the north. 'The coast in the vicinity of Tanga is low, but if the weather is
clear the Bandei mountains, the eastern spurs of the Usambara mountains, which
cover a large tract of country and are about 23 miles inland, will be conspicuous.'
(*Africa Pilot* III, pp. 370–371.)

•55 Pemba Island, 64 kilometres long, with indented bays on the western side.

•56 A 'zavra, zabra', Leitão & Lopes declared simply to be an Arabic embarkation,
used in the transport of cargo in the Mediterranean and Indian Ocean, of whose
characteristics they were ignorant. Ravenstein called it a 'dhow, which is a small
open vessel, sharp at the stern, with a square sail of matting'.

•57 8 April 1498.

•58 The *Encyclopaedia Britannica* (1963) wrote of scurvy, 'a "deficiency" disease,
characterized by debility, blood changes, spongy gums and haemorrhages in the
tissue of the body. It is now known that the cause is deficiency of vitamin C in
the food. This explains the recurrence of scurvy when fresh vegetables or fruit are
unobtainable and its disappearance when they are administered, for these substances
are rich in vitamin C'.

•59 Ravenstein had a footnote: 'Burton suggests that this picture of the Holy Ghost
may have been a figure of Kapot-eshwar, the Hindu pigeon-god and goddess, an
incarnation of Shiva and his wife, the third person of the Hindu triad.'

•60 The form and nature of this 'padrão' is unknown.

•61 Castanheda explained that Vasco da Gama was still hoping to obtain a pilot to
guide the vessels to India. Those engaged in Moçambique were familiar with only
the East African coast.

•62 Ravenstein had a footnote: 'Sir J Kirk suggests to me that these places are
Mtwapa, Takaungu, and Kilifi … Kioni is the usual name of the village usually
called Kilifi.'

•63 15 April.

•64 A balandrau was a gown worn by some religious fraternities; a lambel, a striped cloth used for covering seats and benches.

•65 Ravenstein's comment was: 'Of course, they looked upon these Romish images and pictures as outlandish representations of their gods and idols.'

•66 Ravenstein's footnote: Burton 'suggests that they cried "Krishna", the name of the eighth Incarnation of Vishnu, the second person of the Hindu Trinity, and the most popular of Indian gods'.

•67 The 'Christian' pilot was not Ahmad ibn-Madjid as previously thought. Khoury reported in his *Poem of Sofala* (pp. 19, 20) that Madjid had written in AD 1489 that he had spent 50 years in observation of navigational stars and in 1495 he stressed that he had by far exceeded the age of 60 years, and had reached the end of his life, and was retiring to Arabia. It is possible that a request had been made by Portugal to the 'king' of Malindi to engage an Arabian Sea pilot to lead Gama to Calicut. His name is unknown.

•68 Alcochete, 10 miles up the Tagus, would have been familiar to 'Álvaro Velho of Barreira'.

•69 The south-west monsoon sets in off the East African coast in April, but reaches strength only in May (*Africa Pilot* III, p. 33). The calendar used at the time was still Julian – Portugal adopted the Gregorian in 1582, when 13 days were added overnight. It was accordingly in May (modern time) that the vessels sailed from Malindi and had the advantage of a wind predominantly from astern.

•70 Gama carried a letter from King Manuel to the King of Calicut, thanks to information received from Covilhã.

•71 The coast actually runs south-west to north-east. The 'great bay' was the Arabian Sea, flanked by the horn of Africa, Arabia and Gujerat. Cambay town was at the head of the gulf of that name. Regarding Christians in India, St Thomas according to tradition established churches in south-west India, members of which were persecuted. Bishops reported in 1506 to Constantinople that there were 30 000 Christians in India.

•72 '18' is a correction of the manuscript figure.

•73 Gago Coutinho (I, pp. 411–418) analysed the possible route and found that landfall would have been a mountain in the Ghats, 23 miles north of Calicut.

•74 On 21 May Vasco da Gama sent a 'degredado' ashore to Calicut. He was taken to two Arabs from Tunis who could speak Castilian. They wanted to know why the devil had brought the vessels there. His reply was simple: 'We come in search of Christians and spices.'

The 'king' of Calicut was a petty Hindu ruler entitled Samorim, the sea-raja. He demanded a customary present. The ambassador had no such present, but the captain produced some gifts which were described as paltry and insulting. Gama landed samples of his trade-goods, but these did not excite the Arabs who controlled the commerce of the coast. Members of the expedition continued to consider the Hindu inhabitants of Calicut to be Christians. Many had long beards and long hair; the heads of others were shaved; and many were naked above the waist. The Europeans regarded the local temples as churches.

Much information was gained about the spice trade. To Calicut came pepper, cloves and cinnamon from Ceylon, which was only eight days away. The main source of cloves was Malacca. At Calicut ships were loaded for the Red Sea, from where camels took loads to Alexandria. Also to Alexandria came some goods down the Nile from the lands of Prester John.

On 30 August the vessels sailed from Calicut northwards to the Angediva islands, to be careened and to take on water and fire-wood. They sailed on 5 October on their homeward voyage.

•75 Obviously there was no expert pilot aboard. The vessels should have stayed longer in the Angedivas. 'The N.E. monsoon, which commences in the Arabian sea about the middle of October, sometimes does not reach the coast of Africa and Zanzibar until the middle or end of November: the changes of monsoon, which may occupy a fortnight or more, are accompanied by shifts of wind, calms, squalls of rain, and obscured sky. Occasionally the north-east monsoon is so light that many dhows from Arabia fail to reach Zanzibar ... (*Africa Pilot* III, p. 32).

•76 The manuscript has 'February', a slip presumably by the copyist.

•77 Mogadishu is in latitude 2°02' N.

•78 Pate, on the island of that name, in latitude 2°05' S, was one of the major trading centres on the east coast of Africa.

•79 In 1863 a British naval vessel visited Malindi. The author of *A cruise in the 'Gorgon'* wrote: 'The only things that remind one of those bright days spoken of by Vasco, is the monument, or pillar, built by him on the most prominent extremity of the bay, about forty feet high; once of beautiful white coral, doubtless, but now black and weather-beaten, aged and crumbling; on which, however, like true Englishmen, we carved our names with the point of an Arab's dagger.' The column had been much damaged by wind, sand and sea, and in 1873 the captain of HMS *Briton* reinforced the column with cement. The *Africa Pilot* III (p. 398) stated: 'Between Leopard point and a cliffy point about 1³/₄ miles northward, is a long stretch of sandy beach fronted by reef which dries in places. Vasco da Gama's pillar, a cross, 18 feet (5.5 metres) in height, on the top of which are the arms of Portugal, much weatherworn, stands near the extremity of this cliffy point, at an elevation of 25 feet (7.6 metres).'

In 1959 the present editor and his wife visited Malindi, in the company of James Kirkman, Director of Antiquities in Kenya. Kirkman expressed regret that the cross was of local coral. He was emphatic that it was coral. His two visitors disagreed: they saw stratigraphic lines in the cross, which was also the colour of Lisbon's limestone buildings – and of the Kwaaihoek padrão. The present editor surmounted the beacon and with Kirkman's permission broke off a small chip. This was divided into two. The Director of Geological Services in Kenya declared it was of limestone which did not resemble any of the local coastal limestones, and he regarded it as an import. The Director of Serviços Geologicos de Portugal reported 'its characteristics are very similar to the Turonean limestones of Lisboa'.

•80 Probably Tanga.

•81 Zanzibar lies between 20 and 25 miles from the mainland.

•82 The present editor has searched for fragments of this padrão, but with no success. The name São Jorge came by 1538 to be confined to the northernmost islet, and the southernmost had received the name of São Tiago.

•83 Leitão & Lopes explain that 'achoar' was a Madeiran word which meant to encounter fish on the surface of the water, so these were presumably flying-fish.

•84 In the area of Cape Agulhas the wind in March blows for 55 per cent of the time between north-east and south, with calms for 5 per cent. (*South African Sailing Directions*, I, p. 79.)

•85 Vessels sailing northwards from the Cape of Good Hope have the advantage of the cold Benguela current, and the south-east wind in summer.

•86 The Rio Grande was the estuary of the river Geba, in later Portuguese Guinea. Modern charts show depths of only 11 to 60 fathoms up to 90 miles from the shore.

•87 It is not known for certain why the diary ended. One possibility was that the diarist was a degredado and, without a royal pardon, he disembarked at Santiago.

66 | NOTES

Both the *São Gabriel* and the *Berrio* reached Santiago. There Vasco da Gama ordered Nicolau Coelho to make haste to Portugal to report to King Manuel that the way to India had been opened. Vasco's brother Paulo was desperately ill. Vasco chartered a caravel and sailed to Terceira Island in the Açores (on the usual route from Mina to Portugal). There Paulo died. Nicolau Coelho reached Lisbon on 10 July 1499 and Vasco da Gama at the end of August or the beginning of September.

Castenheda recorded that of the 148 individuals who embarked in 1497 only 55 returned to Portugal. King Manuel in a letter to the Spanish monarchs stated that during the voyage over half the personnel died. But for the surviving Commander, great were the rewards.

Barros wrote that on his return to the Tagus Vasco da Gama 'made his devotions at the house of our Lady of Bethlehem, from which he had started upon this discovery. Here he was visited by all the lords of the court until the day of his entry into the city, which was accompanied by great solemnity, and to celebrate his arrival there were bull fights, theatrical representations, mummeries, and other rejoicings by which the king wished to show his great satisfaction at the illustrious service rendered him by Vasco da Gama, which was one of the greatest ever performed by a subject in so short a time and at so little cost, for through it the king added to his crown ... the titles which it now has of Lord of the Conquest, Navigation, and Commerce of Ethiopia, Arabia, Persia, and India.

'The king further showed his satisfaction and the value he set upon this distinguished service by bestowing the following favours upon Vasco da Gama: that he and his brothers should be called Dom, and that on their escutcheon should be quartered part of the royal arms of the kingdom; he further bestowed upon him the office of the Admiral of the Indian Seas, with a pension of 300,000 reis, and license to trade annually in India with 200 cruzados worth of merchandise, which regularly exchanged for spices yielded in this kingdom, 2,800,000 reis, all this sum being profit: also the title of Vidigueira ...' (trans. GM Theal, *Records of South-Eastern Africa*, VI, Cape Town, 1900, pp. 188–189).

Wind roses in early Portuguese cartography, PMC, *1960, Plate 613.*

Appendix 1

Where was Natal?

The present editor, when at school in Durban in the 1920s, was told that Natal was called Natal because Vasco da Gama was off the Durban Bluff on Christmas Day 1497. During school holidays he often sailed aboard a coaster (of which his father was master) between Durban and Cape Town. He pored over charts, and wondered why there were so many bays and capes that bore the names of saints. Very exciting was especially the return voyage, when advantage was taken of the inshore counter-current, and capes were passed at a distance of only a few cables. Most striking of all was the ruggedness and beauty of the coast about Port St Johns.

The editor-to-be soon found that he was not alone in his appreciation of this stretch of coast and its uniqueness. The *Africa Pilot* III (London, 1929, pp. 134–137) printed: 'Just southward of Rame Head [lat. 31°48' S] a complete change in the general aspect of the country commences. The coast between Rame Head and Waterfall bluff, 32 miles north-eastward, is mainly high and bold, with many outstanding bluffs, and the country appears to be broken into innumerable hills and valleys. Many of the rivers cut through the hills in deep ravines, the sides of which are heavily wooded ....

'Brazen head [lat. 31°44' S] is one of the most conspicuous features of the whole of this part of the coast. There is a clump of trees on its summit, which is 809 feet (246.6 metres) high.' It falls in sheer cliffs to the sea from as much as 500 feet in places. North-eastwards was a peak of 650 feet. This portion of the coast is unmistakable and is rendered more so by the fact that the general aspect of the country changes at Waterfall bluff [15 miles north of Port St Johns].

'The appearance of the land in the neighbourhood of St John River is so remarkable that it is easily recognised from seaward. At the entrance a table mountain, 1 200 feet (365.8 metres) high, appears to have been cleft to its base, leaving a wedge-shaped gap in the centre through which the river discharges into the sea.

'St. John's Gates, the upper part of this tableland, is bare, stratified, sandstone rock, like Table mountain; but, at 200 feet (61 metres) below the summit, a dense forest covers the cliffs to the edge of the river. The western Gate, which is the higher, is very steep; the eastern Gate has two distinct terraces of tableland with grass on them.'

Historical research in Portugal in 1937 quickly shed light on the saintly problem, but that research brought into question Vasco da Gama's coasting and distance run by 25 December. The diarist wrote that 70 leagues had been discovered by that day. Assuming that this was from the Rio do Infante, probably the Keiskama, 'it is impossible to resist the conclusion that it was an exaggeration. The daily run from Mossel Bay to the Infante averaged only 32 or 33 miles … It is unreasonable to suppose that the 240 miles from the Infante northwards, along a coast where the Agulhas current runs if anything more strongly, could be covered at an average of 55 miles a day; except with the assistance of a stronger wind lasting longer than was described in the Roteiro'. (E Axelson, *South-East Africa 1488–1530*, London, 1940, p. 37.) It seemed that the Terra do Natal stretched from Brazen Head past Port St Johns to Waterfall Bluff.

Confirmation of the strength of the Agulhas current came in *South African Sailing Directions* (III, 1985, p. 130): 'Off the coast between Cape Padrone [at the eastern end of Algoa Bay] and Great Fish point [lat. 33°31' S] the Agulhas current sets in a WSW direction parallel with the coast and varying in strength between 1 knot near the coast to 3½ knots or more near the continental shelf. In calm weather the current has been observed running like a race or overfall near the edge of the shelf SE of Cape Padrone.' 'Between Great Fish Point and Port St Johns the width of the continental shelf decreases from about 17 miles off the former to a mere 5 miles off the latter. The Agulhas Current runs roughly parallel to the coast, and is strongest in the vicinity of the shelf edge … Off East London [lat. 33°02' S] the current occasionally attains rates of up to 5 knots, but the average rate during spring and autumn varies between 3 and 3½ knots. During the summer and winter it is usually slightly weaker.' (p. 143)

Resolution of the Christmas problem came with publication of Armando Cortesão and Luís de Albuquerque's *Obras Completas de D. João de Castro* (I, Coimbra, 1968). So spectacular was this landfall, that Castro, one of the most distinguished navigators of the 16th century, made a sketch of it, in 1538 (p. 215). It was of present-day Port St Johns. Castro's pilot told him that he did not know the coast personally, but for some reasons it seemed to him to be the 'primeira terra do Natal' (pp. 212–217). The same day, 2 July, he shot the sun and found the latitude to be 32° S. At the time a good navigator could with a hand-held astrolabe calculate his latitude to within $\frac{1}{3}$ of a degree. (Castro found the latitude of Moçambique to be 14°45' S and the next day 14° and $\frac{5}{6}$. The actual latitude is 15°02' S.)

Further confirmation came from maps and charts. An Italian agent, Cantino, clandestinely bought a copy of the official master world-map kept at the headquarters in Lisbon of the body controlling trade with Guinea and India. The distance between the padrão and 'C: primeir' is the same as that between the padrão and 'C: telhado', the Cape Seal of today. This places Cabo Primeiro as approximately at the Hole-in-the-Wall of today, in latitude 32°02' S, 36 miles south-west of Port St Johns. The southernmost point of Port St Johns is Cape Hermes, in 31°38' S.

Francisco Rodrigues on his chart of 1513 placed Cabo Primeiro at about 32° S; Gaspar Viegas in 1537 at about $31\frac{2}{3}$° S; Diogo Homem in 1581 at about 32° S and in 1568 at about $31\frac{2}{3}$° S, and Lopes, c. 1565, 31° S.

Shipwrecks on the coast, notably of the *São João* in 1552 and the *São Bento* in 1554, prompted João III to order an investigation on how the route to and from India might be made safer and more profitable. One of the recommendations of Pereira Dantas was that the south African coast should be properly explored, and a port found where ships might find sanctuary, effect repairs, load fresh water and wood, and find provisions. There was no immediate action, but in 1574 Manuel de Mesquita Perestrelo received a royal instruction that on his return from captaincy of the Moluccas he was to survey the coast between Cape Correntes and the Cape of Good Hope. There was one particularly good reason why he had been chosen for this duty: he was a survivor of the wreck of the *São Bento*, and had traversed much of that coast on foot. The pilot reckoned the wreck as being at $32\frac{1}{3}$° S. Four hundred and seventy-three persons had boarded the ship in India. Three hundred and twenty-two gained the shore. They decided to walk northwards, towards Moçambique, in the hope that they might find a trading vessel in the river of Lourenço Marques. They did, but only 23 were alive to sail aboard the vessel. One of the few was Mesquita Perestrelo, who wrote a widely read account of the tragic wreck and journey.

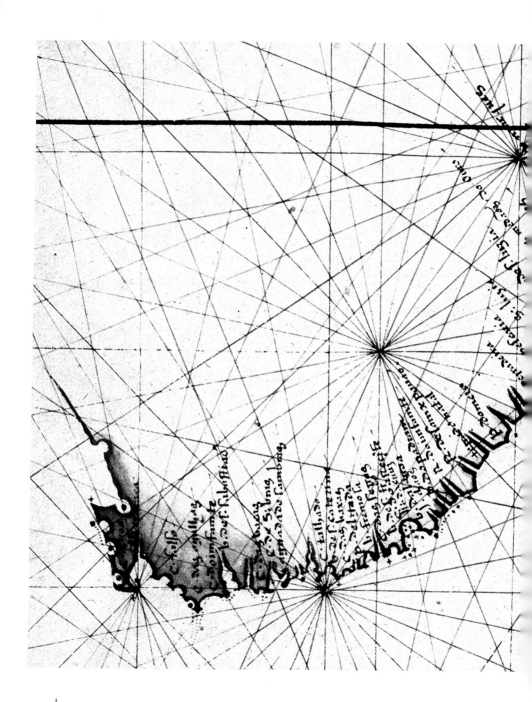

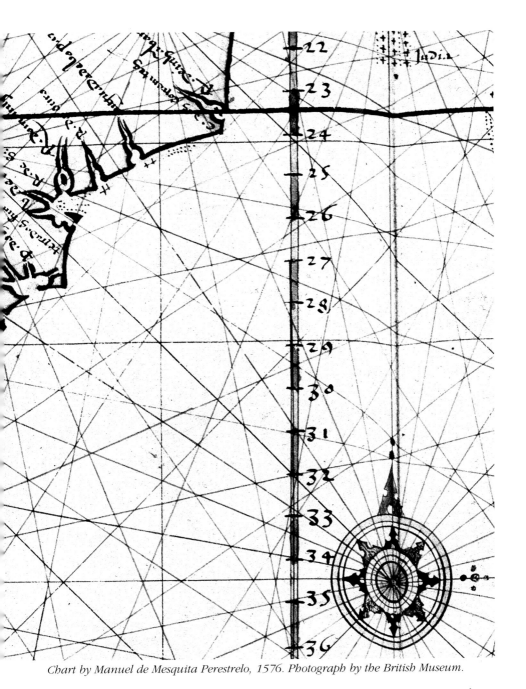

Chart by Manuel de Mesquita Perestrelo, 1576. Photograph by the British Museum.

APPENDIX 1 : WHERE WAS NATAL?

Perestrelo's report was written in Portugal in 1576, in 'a trembling hand' – he was 66 years of age – but the map was firmly drawn, by another person on parchment. He wrote: 'The first point of the land of Natal is in latitude thirty-two degrees ... Its mark of recognition is a great rocky point.' Four 'montes' were to be seen. 'All this land which is called Natal is high, and has patches of sand along the sea. Most of the shore is rocky, and there are reefs. It has no ports. There are in it some rivers, but none capable of receiving large ships. All the sea is deep and clean, only there is a little islet very near the coast ... The appearance of the land for the

Sketch of Ponta Primeira do Natal (First Point of Natal) by João de Castro.

greater part is high and fruitful, and thus it is well peopled and contains a great variety of animals tame and wild.' (Trans. GM Theal, *Records of South-Eastern Africa*, I, Cape Town, 1898, p. 323.) The original report and map are in the British Museum, with later copies in the Biblioteca Publica de Évora.

João de Lisboa in his 'Livro de Marinha' wrote in about 1514 that Ponta Primeira was in latitude 33° S, and Ponta Derradeira, the Last Point of Natal, was in 30^1/$_2$° S (about present Mtwalume). Ogilby, in 1670, showed an

Photograph of Port St Johns by Captain Leith, 1997.

Vasco da Gama
The Diary of His Travels through African Waters 1497–1499

'I Primeira' in about 32° S, and the Derradeira point of Natal in 30° S (15 miles south of Durban). Tirion in an atlas printed in Amsterdam in 1780 showed a very large 'Baai de Natal of Pesqueria', the southern point of which was 'Kaap de Pedras of Pesqueria'.

In 1824 English settlement began at Durban Bay, and in 1827 Wyld published a map which showed Port Natal, Point Natal, St John's River, and south of that 'Natal the first'. 'Coast of Natal' ran north of Port St Johns to Port Natal. Mappers had moved Natal northwards.

Evidence points to Vasco da Gama being off Port St Johns, or in that area, on Christmas Day 1497.

Malindi padrão erected during the return voyage from India. Only the cross remains from the original padrão.

Appendix 2

Vasco da Gama post 1500

Manuel in 1500 dispatched an armada of 15 vessels to India to overawe Muslim traders in Indian waters and establish a fortified trading-station in Calicut. The vessels entered Porto Seguro in Brazil, where Bartolomeu Dias and Nicolau Coelho organised a watering-place (possibly from former knowledge). One vessel was sent back to Portugal with letters that announced this official discovery of Brazil by Portugal. When the fleet was in the southern Atlantic, near the islands soon to be discovered by Tristão da Cunha, a sudden and furious storm sank four vessels, including the caravel of Bartolomeu Dias. At Sofala Cabral was able to oversee repairs to the surviving vessels, but was able to obtain little information on the trade in gold. At the impressive city of Kilwa he met the ruler, each aboard his own boat, side by side, but Ibrahim was naturally reluctant to become a vassal of the distant Portuguese king. Cabral received a great welcome in Malindi and crossed safely to India. He was well received at Cannanor, where a trading station was established. The Samorim of Calicut gave him a royal welcome, and Ayres Correira the factor landed with a number of men to found a station. The number of men is uncertain: one chronicler said 40, another 60, a third 70 and a fourth 100. But the citizens of this wealthy Muslim trading city had no desire to share, let alone surrender, their monopoly of trade. Their anger deepened when Cabral arrested a ship belonging to a prominent citizen. Citizens attacked and killed Correira and some 30 of his men. Cabral promptly seized ten Arab vessels in the port. He found a sympathetic ruler at Cochin and returned to Lisbon in April 1501.

Manuel ordered that Calicut be punished. He organised three armadas to be sent to the East, with Vasco da Gama, Admiral of the East Indian Seas, in command of one of the armadas, and overall commander of the expedition. In command of the second armada was Vicente Sodre, uncle of Vasco da Gama; and the third, of smaller vessels to remain in the East, was under Estevão da Gama, cousin of Vasco da Gama; this left later than the other two.

The ruler of Kilwa gave Vasco da Gama welcome, but refused to subject himself to Portuguese sovereignty. The admiral threatened to bombard the city. The deputy ruler, a wealthy citizen, handed over the required 1 500 miticals of gold, the first of annual tributes to the king of Portugal.

The trading station at Cannanor was supplied, and one established at Cochin. At Calicut Vasco da Gama, obeying orders, waged war without mercy, with grisly mutilations and burnings. There was an eyewitness of this terrorism: a Flemish member of the expedition, who published an account of the expedition's actions in Antwerp in 1504.

Damião de Góis recorded that 'Dom Vasco reached Lisbon with the other ships on the 1st of September 1503. The king, who was in that city at the time, received him with all the rejoicing that his successful voyage deserved, and all the lords and noblemen who were then at court went on board his ship, and afterwards accompanied him to the palace, his page walking before him carrying a basin in which were the two thousand [actually 1 500] miticals of gold, the tribute of the king of Kilwa, and also the agreements which he had made with the latter, and with the kings of Cannanor and Cochin. The king commanded a tabernacle for the blessed sacrament to be made of the said two thousand miticals of gold, ornamented with precious stones, which he commanded to be presented to the monastery of Belem.'

But Góis was wrong. The monstrance, a masterpiece of Portuguese art, was completed in 1506, but it was the property of the king until his death in 1521 when in accordance with his will it passed to the friars of Jeronimos. 'Towards the end of the fifteen hundreds, the monstrance undergoes a transformation, a dome in the shape of a box with circular crystal glasses having been introduced. This dome, which was designed to simplify the use of the artifact, was held fast by two small newels made of gilded silver with engraved decorations and painted enamel applied "cold" over middle-relief facial masks ... There is nothing today to indicate what the original dome of the monstrance might have looked like.' (N Vassallo e Silva, 'The Kilwa Gold', *Oceanos*, April 1992, p. 54.)

Manuel, after Vasco da Gama's return to Portugal in 1499, planned to transform the hermitage at Restelo into a magnificent building. Work began on the foundations that year, and on 8 January 1501 the first stone of the main entrance was laid. Friars took possession of the church and convent in 1551, and the building of this most impressive church of Santa Maria of Belem was finished in 1558.

Vasco da Gama returned to the place of his birth, Sines, on the coast, 88 kilometres south of Lisbon, in 1503, but was not granted the lands which were in the gift of the Order of Santiago and the Sword, and the post of alcaide, which had been promised him when he was a cavalier in that Order – he had switched to the Order of Christ which was favoured by Manuel. He was made a duke, but not granted a dukedom.

In 1509 Francisco de Almeida won a great naval victory over a Turkish fleet. Afonso de Albuquerque captured Goa in 1510, which became Portugal's capital in the East, and Malacca in 1511 – in which year the returning governor, Almeida, and many of his compatriots were killed at the watering place of Saldanha, the later Table Bay. Albuquerque failed to take Aden but was able to control movement up the Persian Gulf by taking Hormuz at its mouth. Portugal became paramount on the northern Indian Ocean.

Vasco da Gama's lack of a dukedom was remedied when he bought Vidigueira, 15 miles from Evora, in 1518, and was granted the title of Conde. Manuel died in 1521, and his son João III surprisingly called on Vasco da Gama to become Viceroy of Portuguese India, which, on paper, extended from the Cape of Good Hope to Malacca. Gama died in India, in Goa, that same year. His reputed bones were entombed in 1880 in the church at Belem, on the site of his departure in 1497 on his historic voyage.

*Monstrance made
from gold brought
from Kilwa by Vasco
da Gama in 1503,
completed in 1506,
and passed to the
friars of Jeronimos in
1521. Now in Museu
Nacional de Arte,
Antiga. Photograph
by Arquivo Nacional
de Fotografia.*

Appendix 3

The voyage and poetry

Vasco da Gama's voyage revolutionised commercial relations between Portugal and the East. It also had intense influence in Portugal on national consciousness – aided, later by Camões, whose day, 10 June, has long been celebrated in Portugal as a national holiday.

Luís Camões, born in about 1524, attended university in Coimbra, where the classics appealed to him in particular. He attended court, but some unexplained affair led to banishment. He became a soldier, and saw action in Ceuta, where he lost an eye. In a brawl in 1552 he wounded a court official, was imprisoned, and released on condition that he serve king and country in the East. He sailed aboard the *São Bento* in 1553. The vessel encountered foul weather, some of it possibly in the vicinity of the Cape of Good Hope. He served in military engagements in Portuguese India. He then took an administrative post in Macau, but this was terminated abruptly. He was summoned back to Goa, but leaving Macau the ship was wrecked and he gained the shore allegedly holding in one hand his as yet uncompleted epic poem.

In Goa Camões was briefly imprisoned, and reduced to penury. He yearned for Portugal, and in 1567 a sympathetic captain enabled him to travel as far as Moçambique. There he lived a pauper's life, but found some solace in completing his great epic poem. He eventually reached Portugal in 1569. He obtained Royal and Inquisitional licence to publish and two editions appeared in 1572 of *Os Lvsiados de Lvis de Camões*. It was a massive, monumental work – 773 pages long.

Vasco Graça Moura sketched the background: 'Camões lived through the final stages of Portuguese expansion and then through the period of decadence and political disintegration of his country. His death, a year or two after the defeat at Alcácer Quibir [in Morocco, where the king Sebastião was killed leading a crusade against a Muslim army], practically coincided with the loss of Portugal's independence to Spain, a situation which lasted until 1640. At the same time, Camões lived in a singular intellectual period of political history.

Vasco da Gama
The Diary of His Travels through African Waters 1497–1499

'The values of classical humanism of the Renaissance which, in the meantime, had spread across Europe from Italy at the end of the 15th century mingled with the doctrines of Erasmus and with debates and conflicts of every kind caused by the Reformation and by the growing theological and practical consolidation of central government. The geographical discoveries brought about a whole new range of information and knowledge about the size of the world and of its real appearance, the discovery of many other peoples, the profusion and variety of cultures and civilizations placed in contact one with another. Coveted merchandise and new riches arrived daily in Europe and the universe was opened up and progressively unveiled. Circulation of the

Portrait of Vasco da Gama, by Gaspar Correa,
Lendas da India *II–II, Lisbon, 1861, facing p. 815.*

printed word increased. All this caused growing concern.' ('Camões and the Discoveries', *Oceanos Portugal and the Sea*, 1992, pp. 44–45.)

To Eduardo Lourenço, 'The Portuguese maritime adventure was modern both in its means and in its results, but paradoxically it was "medieval" in character. By this we mean that it was simultaneously technical, mercantile and religious in character. When Camões wrote his epic a century and a half after the beginnings of maritime exploration, in a context that was already fully modern, this medievalism still dominated his vision of the world. The aim pursued by the Portuguese navigators was tantamount to a crusade.' ('The Lusiads from national epic to universal myth', *The Courier*, Unesco, April 1989, pp. 26–27.)

The *Lusiados* was based on Vasco da Gama's voyage. William Atkinson, who translated the poem into English prose, explained that the name 'means the sons of Lusus, companion of Bacchus and mythical first settler in Portugal: hence, the Portuguese. Virgil, to the Renaissance the greatest among the poets of antiquity, had sung of arms and the man. The *Aeneid* was to Camoens at once model and challenge, but from the opening words he made clear that his would be an *Aeneid* with a difference. "Arms and the men" was his theme, the epic exaltation of a whole race of heroes. What Portugal had accomplished in the East was incomparably greater than the heroic themes of antiquity – and it was true. Nor was it great merely in isolation, the achievement of a handful of stalwarts. It had a national significance, for those stalwarts were the product of all their country's past, and the enterprise was itself but the coping-stone of the logic of that past. And it boasted an even wider significance still, inasmuch as Portugal was engaged in a fight for the true faith, for the spiritual values of Europe, against the forces of error and darkness. It was against this double background that the heroic narrative had to be set, thus involving a range alike in time and in space greater than the career of any one hero could span'. (*Luiz Vaz de Camões (Camoens) Lusiads*, Penguin, London, 1952, pp. 20–22.)

The opening words of the *Lusiads* were: 'This is the story of heroes who, leaving their native Portugal behind them, opened a way to Ceylon, and further, across seas no man had ever sailed before.' But Vasco da Gama traversed those seas only beyond Dias's Rio do Infante, so whilst he and his men were already 'sailing across the restless ocean', up on Olympus Jupiter called an assembly of the gods, and he and Venus agreed that on 'the farthest coast of Africa they would receive a friendly welcome'. In Canto 2 Jupiter foresees a happy future for the travellers. In Cantos 3 and 4 Gama tells the king of Malindi something of the history of Portugal, culminating in the preparations for the expedition, and its departure. In Canto 5 the vessels arrive in St Helena Bay, and Veloso features. The apparition Adamastor appears. Cantos 6 to 8 cover the stay in India. In Canto 8 the weary travellers reach the island of Venus. The final Canto details happy pleasures with the nymphs.

Richard Fanshawe was the first to render the *Lusiados* into English, in 1655. Stanzas from Canto 5 run:

> *To tell thee all the dangers of the deep*
> *(Which humane Judgement cannot comprehend)*
> *Suddain and fearfull storms, the Ayre that sweep;*
> *Lightnings, that with the Ayre the Fire doe blend;*
> *Black Hurracans; thick Nights; Thunder, that keep*
> *The World alarm'd, and threaten the last End:*
> *Would be too tedious: indeed vain and mad,*
> *Though a brasse Tongue, and Iron lungs I had.*

> *I saw those things, which the rude Mariner*
> *(Who hath no Mistresse, but Experience)*
> *Doth for unquestionable Truths aver,*
> *Guided belike by his externall sence:*
> *But Academics (who can never err,*
> *Who by pure Wit, and Learning's quintessence,*
> *Into all Nature's secrets dive and pry)*
> *Count either Lyes, or coznings of the Eye.*

> ...

> *If old Philosophers (who travayld through*
> *So many Lands, her secrets out to spye)*
> *Had viewed the Miracle which I did view,*
> *Had sayled with so many winds as I;*
> *What writings had they left behind! what new,*
> *Both Starres, and Signs, bequeath'd to Us! What high*
> *And strong Influxes! What did Qualities!*
> *And all pure Truths, without allay of Lyes!*

(From Luís F Barreto, *Portugal: Pioneiro do Diálogo Norte/Sul*, Lisbon, 1988, p. 131.)

*Luis de Camões. Portrait by Fernão Gomes. In Arquivo Nacional da Torre do Tombo.
From* Portugal Language and Culture, *Commission of Portugal for the Seville Universal
Exhibition 1992, p. 42.*

Very pertinent lines penned by Fanshawe described the inhabitants of later Mossel Bay:

> *Upon the sandy beach, with cheerfulness*
> *They meet us, and Dances Festival.*
> *With them, their Wives: and their mild flocks of Sheep,*
> *Which fat and faire, and frisking they did keep.*

> *Their Wives upon straw-Pillions (black as Jet)*
> *Slow-paced Oxen (like Europa) ride:*
> *Beasts, upon which a higher price they set*
> *Then all the Cattle of the Field beside.*
> *Sweet madrigalls (in Ryme or Prose compleat,*
> *In their own Tongue) to rustick-Reed apply'de,*
> *They sing in Parts, as gentle Shepherds use,*
> *That imitates of Tytirus the Muse.*

(From Stephen Gray, *Camoens and the Poetry of South Africa*, Camoens Annual Lectures No. 1, Oppenheimer Institute for Portuguese Studies, Johannesburg, 1980, p. 5.)

Vasco da Gama inspired many South African poets. One was 'W', probably
John Wheatley, who in 1830 published 'The Cape of Storms'; it started:

Spirit of Gama! round the stormy Cape,
Bestriding the rude whirlwind as thy steed;
The thunder cloud, thy car, thy spectre shape
Gigantic; who upon the gale dost feed
And drink the water spout; thy shroud, the skies;
Thy sport, the South and vast Atlantic sea;
Thine eye, the light'ning's flash! – Awake! arise
From out the deep, in dread and awful sov'reignty!

Now hast thou risen! By heaven it is a sight
Most God-like, grand, and glorious to behold;
Three elements contend, and fierce in fight
As those who warr'd with mighty Jove of old.
Oh, God! If any doubt thy being, or rate
With vain and impious mind at nought thy pow'r,
So may it be such daring sceptic's fate
To pass the Cape of Storms, when angry tempests lower.

(M van Wyk Smith, *Shades of Adamastor*, p. 74.)

Vasco da Gama

The Diary of His Travels through African Waters 1497–1499

DCF Moodie published 'Adamastor, or the Titan shape of the mighty Cape' in 1887. It began:

> *Of old the Titans, in unholy rage,*
> *Waged impious war against the thunderer Jove;*
> *And oft we've seen along the classic page*
> *How – lightning armed – the 'Cloud Compeller' hove*
> *The rebels headlong down to earth, where still they strove*
> *Awhile amongst themselves, and were doomed*
> *To lone and distant spots, ne'er more to rove,*
> *But stand the sentries grim where breakers boomed;*
> *Where lay life's light, and joy, and Hope itself entombed.*

> *The youngest Titan, Adamastor named*
> *(So sings in sweetest strain the Lusian bard),*
> *Was banished south to far off country, claimed*
> *In after days, by Diaz, sailor hard –*
> *And here to-day the Giant stands – ill starred –*
> *His human semblance altered, and his brow,*
> *Tho' princely still, all wild, and fiercely scarred.*
> *But as of yore he stood, so stands he now,*
> *And sadly prays to Jove to change his vengeful vow.*

But Jove has other work, and will not hear,
And Adamastor prays in vain, but yet
O'er the wild Ocean doth the Monster rear
His lofty crest of crags, and front of jet.
And mark, oh mark! the noble profile set
In sternest beauty o'er the western wave –
(His forehead still with sylphlike wreathings wet)
And see the Monarch gaze where Sol doth lave
His crimson head in billow blue – his daily grave.

Yes, o'er that wave did Adamastor scan
Th' intrepid Diaz, and De Gama bold
Pursue their dubious course with tools and plan
Of rudest sort, but still with courage bold
Their way to lands possess'd of fabled gold;
And from their high and clumsy vessels saw
A lofty land where mists fantastic rolled,
And storms resounding from the 'caverned shore,'
With hollow groan 'repeat the tempest's (horrid) roar.'

(From van Wyk Smith, *Shades of Adamastor*, pp. 80–81.)

'JR' composed 'Vasco da Gama (Christmas 1497)', published in 1907.
It opened with:

They were sick at heart and weary, they were tired of wind and wave,
They saw no beauty in the sea, it seemed to them their grave;
Two moons had grown and gone again since they had looked their last
Upon the mount whose beetling brow braves the Antarctic blast;
Morn after morn had found them still one speck upon the sea,
Eve after eve had left them yet all landless on the lee:
And ever as the day arrived more sad, and stern, and strange
The ocean seemed to be to them; it bore no other change.
And ever as the night came more lonely, lost and drear
Those seamen felt, as northward, ho! their course they strove to steer.

(From *Shades of Adamastor*, p. 91.)

Lance Fallow's 'Land's End of Africa', 1909, began:

> *The spirit of the Stormy Cape,*
> *That frowned on Vasco's ships,*
> *Still wears at times that dreadful shape*
> *And speaks with threatening lips.*

> *Still when the wild north-westers blow,*
> *The sea's foundations shake,*
> *And forth the surging squadrons go*
> *Some shattered breach to take.*

> *But when the breath of quietude*
> *Is felt against the brow,*
> *Ah, then 'tis fairyland renew'd*
> *By more than wizard's vow.*

> *Then, by the stainless alchemy*
> *Of sun and breeze and air,*
> *A purer radiance fills the sky*
> *Than sense may fully bear.*

> *The mountain, like a temple-porch,*
> *Its own true glory hath,*
> *Lit by the morning's incense-torch*
> *That shows our winding path.*

(From *Shades of Adamastor*, p. 98.)

The noblest South African translation of the *Lusiados* has been that by Guy Butler. He graphically described the appearance of Adamastor (in Canto 5, stanzas 37–43):

From there, after the circling sun had seen
Our ship five times; while sailing gently through
Those seas where other ships had never been;
While steadily the following wind still blew,
And while beneath a starry sky serene
We kept watch in the prow with other crew –
Suddenly a cloud, darkening all the air
Congealed above our masts and hovered there.

So sinister a shade its coming bore
That through our quickened pulses terror spread
The great waves thundered and we heard them roar
Crashing far off upon a rocky head.
I cried, 'O heavenly Powers whom I adore,
What threat divine is this? What secret dread
Now stalks this dismal realm? It shows a form
Of something far more terrible than storm.'

While I yet spake, under that tenebrous cowl
A horrid form took shape before our gaze:
A figure huge and vigorous, with heavy jowl
And unkempt beard, whose sullen eyes, ablaze
From caves beneath the beetling forehead, scowl
With hate enough to frighten and amaze –
Grey, and matted with clay his shock of hair;
Yellow in his black mouth his teeth appear;

Vasco da Gama

The Diary of His Travels through African Waters 1497–1499

So vast his limbs and such a height he showed
He must be second only in his size
To that colossal statue of old Rhodes,
A wonder of the world to ancient eyes;
His voice vibrates and, quivering, forebodes;
From subterranean deeps it seems to rise.
To hear and see him there, upon that deep,
Made each scalp tingle and our flesh to creep.

'O race!' he cried, 'more daring than any yet
In undertaking ventures such as these,
Who, from lost wars and causes cruel though great,
And hopeless labours, never will rest at ease;
Since these forbidden bounds you violate
And dare to trespass on my secret seas, –
These seas long held by me, by me alone
Against all seamen whom the world has known, –

Since you have come to search and desecrate
The mysteries of nature and the main,
To knowledge of which no being ever yet,
Human or immortal could attain, –
Now hear me tell what vengeance future Fate
Holds for your conquests and your glories vain:
Whether on waters vast, or on the land
Which you by sword or fire will command –

Know that all ships that thus far shall intrude,
Daring to make the voyage that you now dare,
Shall be afflicted in this latitude
With storms and hurricanes too hard to bear;
On the first fleet that, through these waters rude
Following your wake, presumes to steer
I'll strike with such harsh force they shall forget
In present pain the terrors of this threat.'

(From *Lantern*, Jan. 1988, p. 18, with Guy Butler's permission.)

92 | APPENDIX 3 : THE VOYAGE AND POETRY

Roy Campbell wrote (in *Portugal*, London, 1957, pp. 136, 143): 'At the outbreak of the last war I sailed from Lisbon to volunteer for the British Army, and spent all the money I had on the complete poems of Camões, which I eventually carried in my kitbag round the Cape and out east to many of the very places described in the Lusiads, such as Mombaça, Melinde, Lama: but the most extraordinary coincidence was to be posted, when unfit for more active service, opposite the very spot where he wrote the most affecting of his *Canções*; apparently he was coast-watching for Arab dhows, as I was for Jap submarines, which often camouflaged themselves as dhows, to come in close, as did the one that loosed an aeroplane over Mombaça.' 'Camões is the one to enchant stagnant, dead hours in malarial swamps, or endless dusty days on desert promontories, and after a couple of years with him, I wrote the following sonnet to express the real comradeship he finally inspires: it expresses that feeling better than could be done in prose.'

> *Camões, alone, of all the lyric race,*
> *Born in the black aurora of disaster,*
> *Can look a common soldier in the face:*
> *I find a comrade where I sought a master:*
> *For daily, while the stinking crocodiles*
> *Glide from the mangroves on the swampy shore,*
> *He shares my awning on the dhow, he smiles,*
> *And tells me that he lived it all before.*
> *Through fire and shipwreck, pestilence and loss,*
> *Led by the ignis fatuus of duty*
> *To a dog's death – yet of his sorrows king –*
> *He shouldered high his voluntary Cross,*
> *Wrestled his hardships into forms of beauty,*
> *And taught his gorgon destinies to sing.*

(From *Talking Bronco*, Faber & Faber, 1946, p. 11.)

Earlier, in *Adamastor*, 1930, Roy Campbell came out with what Gray called 'One of the key interpretations of Adamastor for our time' (Gray, p. 10):

Rounding the Cape

> *The low sun whitens on the flying squalls,*
> *Against the cliffs the long grey surge is rolled*
> *Where Adamastor from his marble halls*
> *Threatens the sons of Lusus as of old.*

> *Faint on the glare uptowers the dauntless form,*
> *Into whose shade abysmal as we draw,*
> *Down on our decks, from far above the storm,*
> *Grin the stark ridges of his broken jaw.*

> *Across his back, unheeded, we have broken*
> *Whole forests: heedless of the blood we've spilled,*
> *In thunder still his prophecies are spoken,*
> *In silence, by the centuries, fulfilled.*

> *Farewell, terrific shade! though I go free*
> *Still of the powers of darkness art thou Lord:*
> *I watch the phantom sinking in the sea*
> *Of all that I have hated or adored.*

> *The prow glides smoothly on through seas quiescent:*
> *But where the last point sinks into the deep,*
> *The land lies dark beneath the rising crescent,*
> *And Night, the Negro, murmurs in his sleep.*

(From *Shades of Adamastor*, p. 111.)

Another great South African poet was Sydney Clouts. His 'The Discovery' was a masterpiece of brevity:

> *The heartbeat! the heartbeat! Be,*
> *but, if, how, when, between.*
> *Every drop of blood speaks by,*
> *the soul in concept*
> *storms the strings.*
>
> *Here's the expedition, knot by knot,*
> *the rigging and the prow.*
>
> *Canary Islands, brightly;*
> *Bojador, in darkness*
> *darkness*
> *esperança!*
>
> *Rounding the Cape, the sodden*
> *wooden grumble of the wheel.*

(From *English in Africa*, Grahamstown, Oct. 1984, pp. 127–128.)

The voyage of Vasco da Gama both excited and saddened Fernando Pessoa, considered by many to be the greatest modern Portuguese poet. He was born in Lisbon. His stepfather was appointed Portuguese consul in Durban. Pessoa attended Durban High School – where he was doubtless informed that Vasco da Gama was off the Durban Bluff on Christmas Day 1497 – from 1899 to 1902. He had to learn a foreign language, but a term report in 1901, when he was two years younger than the average age of the class, declared him to be 'Very good' in two subjects, 'Excellent' in two, and in the other two 'Brilliant'. A master wrote of him a few years later: 'His English composition was always very good and sometimes approached genius.' When he was 13 he wrote a poem entitled 'Anamnesis'; 'What other boy of 13 would have heard of the word?' asked HD Jennings ('Four old reports', *NEON*, Pietermaritzburg, Dec. 1986, pp. 12–20). In 1903 he won the Queen Victoria Memorial prize for an English essay – first of 899 candidates. One of his best known poems is 'The Portuguese Sea':

O salty sea, how much of your salt
Are tears of Portugal!
For us to sail you, how many mothers cried,
How many sons prayed in vain!
How many brides stayed unmarried
Just for you to be ours, oh sea!

Was it worth it? Everything is worthwhile
If the soul is not mean.
Whoever wants to sail beyond the Bojador
Must go beyond anguish.
God gave the sea danger and depth
But in it mirrored the sky.

(Trans. FEG Quintanilha, *Fernando Pessoa Sixty Portuguese Poems*, University of Wales Press, Cardiff, 1971, p. 47.)

Another is 'Padrão', dated 1918:

Great is the effort, small is the man.
I, Diogo Cão, navigator, left
This padrão beside the golden sands
And sailed forth.

Divine is the soul, unfinished is the work.
This padrão tells the wind and the skies
That of the daring task my part is done:
The future is up to God.
And the Quinas [the five shields on the royal arms] which you see here
Teach the large and conceivable ocean
That the bounded sea can be Greek or Roman:
But the sea without end is Portuguese.

And at the top, the cross tells that what I have
In my soul and urges me to sail
Will find only in the eternal peace of God
The illusive harbour.

(From Quintanilha, p. 41.)

Artist's impression of what Vasco da Gama's ship, São Gabriel, *probably looked like, based on sketches of ships on early 16th-century maps and on research by Jaìme Martins Barata.*

Index

Back cover:
Vasco da Gama Museum at Shelley Point.

Bibliography

- Abreu, Lisuarte, *Livro de Lisuarte de Abreu*, Lisbon, 1992.
- *Africa Pilot* III, London, 1929.
- Andrade, Freire de, trans., *Documentos sobre os Portugueses em Moçambique e na Africa Central* ... I, Lisbon, 1962.
- Atkinson, W, *Luiz Vaz de Camões (Camoens) Lusiads*, London, 1952.
- Axelson, E, *South-East Africa 1488–1530*, London, 1940.
- -----------, ed., *South African Explorers*, Oxford, 1954.
- -----------, *Congo to Cape: Early Portuguese Explorers*, London, 1973.
- -----------, *Portuguese in South-East Africa 1488–1600*, Johannesburg, 1973.
- -----------, *The Dias Voyage, 1487–1488: Toponymy and Padrões*, Centro de Estudos de História e Cartografia Antiga 189, Lisbon, 1988.
- -----------, ed., *Dias and his Successors*, Cape Town, 1988.
- Barata, JM, *O Navio "São Gabriel" e as Naus Manuelinas*, AECA, Vol. XXXIX, Coimbra, 1970.
- Barker, RA, 'Of caravelas, tides and water', *Stvdia* 54/55, pp. 101–121, Lisbon, 1996.
- Barreto, Luís F, *Portugal: Pioneiro do Diálogo Norte/Sul*, Lisbon, 1988.
- Barros, João de, *Asia de Joam de Barros* ..., I, Coimbra, 1930.
- -----------, trans. GM Theal, *Records of South-Eastern Africa*, VI, Cape Town, 1900.
- Brochado, Costa, *O Piloto Arabe de Vasco da Gama*, Lisbon, 1982.
- Campbell, Roy, *Adamastor*, London, 1930.
- -----------, *Talking Bronco*, London, 1946.
- -----------, *Portugal*, London, 1957.
- Chumovsky, TA, *Três Roteiros Desconhecidos de Ahmad ibn-Madjid* ... Moscow, Leningrad, 1957.
- Congresso Internacional de História dos Descobrimentos, *Actas II*, Lisbon, 1961.
- Cortesão, Armando, and Mota, Avelino Teixeira da, *Portvgaliae Monvmenta Cartographica,* Vol. I–V, Lisbon, 1960.
- Cortesão, Armando, and Albuquerque, Luís de, *Obras Completas de D. João de Castro*, I, Coimbra, 1968.
- -----------, *History of Portuguese Cartography*, I, Coimbra, 1969.
- -----------, *The Mystery of Vasco da Gama*, Coimbra, 1973.
- Costa, A Fontoura da, *Às portas da India em 1484*, Lisbon, 1936.
- -----------, *O descobrimento do Brasil*, Lisbon, 1961.
- Costa, Gomes da, *Descobrimentos e Conquistas*, II, Lisbon, 1928.
- Coutinho, Gago, 'Reconstituição da Rota seguido por Vasco da Gama', *Diário da Viagem de Vasco da Gama*, Vol. II, Porto, 1945.
- -----------, *A Náutica dos Descobrimentos: Os Descobrimentos Maritmos vistos por um Navegador Colectânea* ... ed. Moura Braz, Vol. II, Lisbon, 1952.
- Crawford, OGS, *Ethiopian Itineraries circa 1400–1524*, London, 1958.
- Devereux, WC, *A cruise in the 'Gorgon'*, London, 1869.

- *Documents on the Portuguese in Mozambique and Central Africa 1497–1840,* Vol. I (1497–1506), Lisbon, 1962.
- Forbes, Vernon, 'Colonel RJ Gordon at the Dias Cross, Kwaaihoek 1786', *Quarterly Bulletin of the South African Library,* Cape Town, September 1972.
- *História da Colonização Portuguesa do Brasil,* Vol. I, Porto, 1921.
- *História da Colonização Portuguesa do Brasil,* Vol. II, Porto, 1923.
- Khoury, Ibrahim, *As-Sufaliyya "The poem of Sofala" by Ahmad ibn Magid,* CECA CXLVIII, Coimbra, 1983.
- Kimble, G, trans. and ed., *Esmeraldo de Situ Orbis,* Hakluyt Society, 1937.
- Kopke, Diogo, and Paiva, A da Costa, *Roteiro da Viagem que em Descobrimento da India Pelo Cabo da Boa Esperança fez Dom Vasco da Gama em 1497,* Porto, 1838.
- Leitão, Humberto, and Lopes, Vicente, *Dicionário da Linguagem de Marinha Antiga e Actual,* Lisbon, 1974.
- Leite, Duarte, *História dos Descobrimentos,* Lisbon, 1958.
- Ley, CD, *Portuguese Voyages 1498–1663,* London, 1947.
- Lourenço, Eduardo, 'The Lusiads from national epic to universal myth', *The Courier,* Unesco, April 1989, pp. 26–27.
- Marques, Alfredo Pinheiro, *Portvgaliae Monvmenta Cartographica, Vol. VI, Adenda ...,* Lisbon, 1987.
- -----------, *Portugal and the Discovery of the Atlantic,* Lisbon, 1990.
- -----------, *A Maldição da Memória do Infante Dom Pedro e as origens dos Descobrimentos Portugueses,* Figueira da Foz, 1994.
- -----------, *Vida e Obra do 'Principe Perfeito' Dom João II,* Figueira da Foz, 1997.
- Peres, Damião, *História dos Descobrimentos Portugueses,* Porto, 1943.
- Perestrelo, Manuel de Mesquita, trans. GM Theal, *Records of South-Eastern Africa, I,* Cape Town, 1898.
- Quintanilha, FEG, ed. and trans., *Fernando Pessoa Sixty Portuguese Poems,* Cardiff, 1971.
- Ravenstein, EG, *Vasco da Gama's First Voyage,* London, 1898.
- Smith, Andrew and Pasche, WE, 'Balthasar Springer at the Cape (1506)', *Quarterly Bulletin of the South African Library,* March 1997, pp. 93–98.
- Smith, M van Wyk, *Shades of Adamastor Africa and the Portuguese connection: An anthology of poetry,* Grahamstown, 1988.
- [Velho, Álvaro] *Diário da Viagem de Vasco da Gama,* intro. by Damião Peres, Porto, 1945.
- Tibbetts, GR, *The navigational theory of the arabs in the fifteenth and sixteenth centuries,* AECA, Vol. XXXVI, Coimbra, 1969.